THE
REINVENTIONIST
MINDSET

Joe Jackman

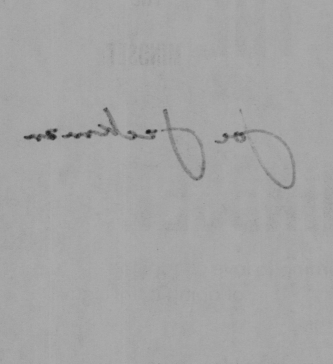

Joe Jackman

THE REINVENTIONIST MINDSET

Learning to love change,
and the human how of doing it brilliantly

Foreword by Joe Mimran

PAGE TWO
BOOKS

Cataloguing in publication information is available from Library and Archives Canada.

ISBN 978-1-989025-92-5 (hardcover)
ISBN 978-1-989025-93-2 (ebook)

Page Two
www.pagetwo.com

Jacket and interior design by Peter Cocking
Printed and bound in Canada by Friesens
Distributed in Canada by Raincoast Books
Distributed in the US and internationally by
Publishers Group West, a division of Ingram

20 21 22 23 24   5 4 3 2 1

joejackman.com

Contents

Foreword

T'S 2002, AND I am sitting on a couch in the corner of a lounge area at my daughter's school, during a father/daughter dance event. At the other end of the couch is John Lederer, then President of the Canadian retail behemoth Loblaw Companies Limited. We had met several years before, when the Loblaw real estate department had reached out to enquire about Club Monaco. At the time I was President as well as Founder, and Loblaw was interested in including the brand in one of their retail developments. Instead, we went on to create and open a breakthrough lifestyle store called Everyday Living, the genesis for what would later become the retail chain Caban. Lederer knew when we met that I had sold Club Monaco—what had by then become a hugely successful apparel chain—to Ralph Lauren a few years prior, and was curious as to what my plans were. I shared that I had returned to the entrepreneurial world, becoming a consultant and exploring a number of ventures. Hearing this, he asked a simple question: "Would you consider designing twenty home and kitchen items under the President's Choice brand?" I went on to create PC Home, a line of thoughtfully designed and affordable houseware items under the legendary food brand President's Choice. So began a journey that would lead me to the two Joe's . . . Joe Fresh, what would become the fastest-growing brand of affordable style in Canada and ultimately my namesake brand, and Joe Jackman.

As those who know me would attest, I'm not a pushover when it comes to branding and every aspect of design specification. I built my career on understanding the power of design and how to use it to build true brand distinction. How it is essential to not only creating meaningful differentiation, but more broadly, how it can reframe customer perception of entire categories of goods. When the opportunity of creating a new apparel line for Loblaw arose, I had some very strong opinions on not just the design of the product I was tapped to create and source, but also on everything to do with the brand: the name and image, the photography style, how it would show up in-store, packaging details, and launch communications right down to the fonts. Well, as it turns out, so did Jackman. When I was first asked to work with him on the creation of the brand beyond the product itself—he at the time a strategic creative consultant to Loblaw—I expected I could either listen to what he had to say or completely ignore it, depending on whether I agreed with his thinking. This was not to be however, as within a few months he crossed over from consultant to Loblaw's new head of national Marketing responsible for taking Joe Fresh to market. In other words, he became a key collaborator and fellow decision maker in the process. Given that I was waist-deep in designing, sourcing, and operationalizing a new brand from scratch, this was a complication I could do without.

What struck me first about Jackman was how, behind his easy-going and affable style, there was a tenacity and belief in his work. It reminded me of, well, me. It followed that we of course bucked heads on everything from logo design and model selection to marketing tactics. Yet there was one thing we were 100 percent aligned on: Joe Fresh would come out of the gate fully formed, with a distinct voice and point of view that would compel customers to visit and buy. What made this bold was that it was counter to the prevailing thinking at the time, namely that customers would shop Joe Fresh while shopping for groceries. We quietly agreed that, when we were done, the opposite would be true. Customers and non-customers alike would make special trips to Loblaw stores to shop Joe Fresh, and pick up some groceries and home goods while they were there. *Joe Fresh would become a destination brand.*

From a less than smooth start, this was the beginning of a wonderful collaboration between "the Joes" that carries on to this day. We were both passionate in the belief that there was always a better and more creative way to do things. We were intent on proving that a deep customer understanding and focus combined with strategic creativity would deliver sustainable results. And, we learned a valuable lesson in how important it is to achieve buy-in at every level of an organization—that by engaging and inspiring people in creative, strategic, *and* disarmingly human ways, the odds of success are greatly increased.

Joe Fresh became the number one apparel brand in Canada in units and dollars, an amazing success. I had heard about the superb transformation Jackman had gone on to tackle at Duane Reade in New York, so I called him to ask if he was interested in another project. This brought about our collaboration on the creation of the Dip brand for Kroger (at $120 billion in sales, the world's largest grocer). It was John Lederer (that name again) who put us together on the Staples transformation, with Jackman Reinvents tapped for strategy and customer experience and me and my team contributing product design. Where once there was uncertainty— *Do I really need this guy involved?*—now there was confidence and excitement at the possibility of further collaborations.

I share these thoughts with you for one reason: if you are a leader at any level of an organization, or an entrepreneur, this book is a must-read. You already know the world is changing fast. You hopefully appreciate the importance of design and creativity in the commercial act of setting a business course and bringing it to life. Now, you need to learn how to do it all brilliantly, quickly, and *humanly*. As a Dragon on CBC Television's hit show *Dragons' Den*, I was always emphasizing the importance of understanding the true needs of the customer, and how to differentiate a product or service. I have always worked intuitively, synthesizing great design and taste, looking at consumer trends, and capitalizing on those unmet needs. Yet Joe Jackman's "secret sauce," which he shares in *The Reinventionist Mindset*, opened my mind to new and thoughtful ideas on making change and getting it to stick.

All strategies ultimately lose their relevance. For those who intend to not only survive but thrive by creating change, *The Reinventionist Mindset* is a distillation of lessons learned and built upon, delivered in an easy-to-read form, with practical ideas for charting your own course. Consider it an antidote to the inevitability of failure and an opportunity to actively embrace your future.

Joe Mimran

Co-Founder & Chairman, Gibraltar & Co.;
Founder of Club Monaco, Joe Fresh;
former Dragon, *Dragons' Den*

PART ONE

CHANGE
IS
GOOD

1

Not quite normal

I T'S THE SUMMER of 1970, and I'm spending it with my older sisters at the University of Windsor. Lucky me. The last of six kids, on leave from life with my open-minded parents. Open-minded because few kids my age are spending their school break in an old mansion with a group of twenty-something students. I'm wide-eyed and wild-haired and soaking it all up.

Like university cities everywhere, Windsor is a hotbed of unrest. America is just across the Detroit River, Nixon is the U.S. President, and the Vietnam War rages. Peace rallies, union picket lines, and sit-ins are the daily norm, and I've got a front-row seat on an intense yet exciting world dramatically different from the one I'm used to. My sisters take me to meetings with their friends—romantic idealists each and every one—and I hear heady ideas about change: How it is coming. That it is upon us. That the status quo is the enemy, and it is up to us to tear it down and rebuild it. I am thoroughly inspired. I am passionately swept up by the idea of purposeful change. I am ten years old.

What's in the hat?

The "status quo" is a Latin expression meaning the way things are, quite literally translated as "the state in which." Most often used in a social or political context, the phrase carries a heavy connotation of thinking and behavior fixed in time, a state of being that is unlikely to change without some kind of strenuous intervention. But even at the age of ten, my understanding of it was completely upside-down. At best, the status quo in my world then was a fluid idea, a point in time in some kind of ever-changing continuum. For example, if anyone in my family didn't like the way things were, we were encouraged to speak up and suggest another way. If my siblings or I, four girls and two boys, had an idea, there was a forum—an actual *process*—where we were ensured a fair hearing: The Family Meeting.

Family Meetings took place most Sundays after dinner. Mom, Dad, and the kids would gather to discuss whatever was on our minds. If there were too many agenda items, as was almost always the case, the revolving chairperson (I recall my first turn at the age of seven, with a little help from my older sisters) would draw topics from a hat, and one by one we would tackle them together. Sometimes tame, sometimes outlandish, we would debate and disagree until eventually we aligned, an experiment in democracy closer to Greek or Roman times than the typical family dynamic of the day. In those moments, we were *peers* and not a hierarchy. Given that the age range from oldest to youngest participant was a full fifty years, this was a remarkable sharing of power by my parents, more proof of their open-mindedness. In those moments we felt a common sense of purpose, and a collective responsibility to make things better. At its heart that meant not holding on to the way things were, regardless of how comfortable we might be. It was incredibly empowering. Suffice it to say, the status quo never stood a chance. Only later did I realize how weird it was by anyone else's standard. Growing up, change wasn't difficult or scary. Change was just a conversation. An examination of possibilities and trade-offs. The difference between what *is* and what *could be* was a fulsome debate followed by participative decision. Did I love and agree with every one of those decisions? No. But at least I had a say, and that meant every decision was as much mine as anyone else's. Nothing was being *done* to me. And, because I knew why every choice was made and felt a part of it, I got behind each and every decision and helped make it a reality.

Another round of Manhattans

Fast-forward forty years and I am in New York, too tired and too many cocktails into a serious celebration to fully grasp the consequence of the moment. The picture I snap on my iPhone—taken in Times Square at 10 p.m., February 17, 2010—shows a 100-foot-high digital screen that reads, "Welcome Duane Reade into the Walgreens family." As strategic advisor and acting Chief Marketing Officer of Duane Reade, the landmark drugstore chain on practically every corner in New York, I had been up all night with the Walgreens team putting final touches on that morning's media messaging. The press release crossed the wire at 8 a.m., followed by a blur of staff briefings and media events, marking what would be considered one of the highest-profile saves in American retail history.

Bloomberg Businessweek called it "Duane Reade's Miracle Makeover," as in a few short years it moved from one list—the list of daily grievances on the popular duanereadesucks.blogspot.com—to another better list—the annual "Best of New York" published by *New York Magazine*. Even the cover of *Mergers & Acquisitions* magazine, the go-to journal of the private equity crowd, featured a photo of a new Duane Reade store in the SoHo district of Manhattan with the accompanying headline "Vindicated!" This wasn't just a New York tale of big, bold change in the biggest, boldest metropolis on the planet, it was a poster example of what successful reinvention looks and feels like.

Four decades apart, from ten years old to fifty years old, the line between these life-defining moments is a straight if not quite normal one, and for me it came with a soundtrack. The relentless drumbeat that marched me from Winnipeg, where I was born, to Windsor, where I was radicalized, to London, where I was schooled, to Toronto, where I began my career, and on to New York...the urgent pulse that pushed me forward, from impressionable boy to designer to creative director to strategist to corporate executive, and finally, to Reinventionist...was CHANGE. Change... *bang*...is...*bang*...GOOD.

2

Change in sixteen words

OOGLE THE WORD "change" and up comes 15.9 billion citations. Amongst the many references are quotations from some of history's greats, from Gandhi ("Be the change you wish to see in the world") and Tolstoy ("Everyone thinks of changing the world, but no one thinks of changing himself") to Warhol ("They always say time changes things, but you actually have to change them yourself") to my personal favorite, Einstein ("The world as we have created it is a process of our thinking. It cannot be changed without changing our thinking"). If change is on your mind, as it has been on mine since I was a child, then it is worth some time exploring what change actually *is*. Dictionary.com defines "change" as "to make the form, nature, content, future course, etc., of (something) different from what it is or from what it would be if left alone." Moreover, it is difficult to do—"We underestimate the process," is reason number six on *Psychology Today*'s "8 Reasons Why It's Really So Hard to Change Your Behavior." But with full acknowledgment of how foolhardy it may be to attempt to summarize 16 billion data points and centuries worth of commentary, here are the sixteen words that best sum it up for me:

Change is hard yet essential.
Everything tends to work out if you get good at it.

Both points, as you will discover in this book, are true. The first one is fairly obvious: Change is necessary because nothing is immune from the need for it—not companies, not brands, not people. The second point is not so obvious. It is the action part. The part that links what's happening with what to do about it. As with most worthwhile things in life, it is an acquired skill. Anyone can learn to make change brilliantly (as Chef Gusteau claims in *Ratatouille*, "Anyone can cook!"), and now is definitely the time to learn how to do it.

Shorter and faster

Being good at change matters more today simply because change itself is coming more quickly. What was once an occasional need for substantial change over the course of a business or lifetime—with plenty of time in between the "big change moments"—is now occurring more frequently, and the facts bear that out.

Unlike our grandparents and parents, we are now more mobile. We're likely to live not just in one place but many over a lifetime; living in one city and working in another, or having family spread out across the globe. Relocating is a very big change moment, shown by research to be one of life's most stressful. The odds of having more than one career today are also higher, partly enabled by longer life spans. Career transitions are amongst the list of angst-inducing big change moments.

It is the same commercially. Brand and business life cycles are shorter, and so is the average tenure of executives. What used to go on for decades in my dad's generation—careers, companies, categories—can now be counted in years and sometimes months. Today, the life span of an athletic shoe design is thirty days, and, according to the global "fast fashion" retailer Zara, there are no longer four seasons for apparel, but fifty-two micro-seasons, with fresh new waves of product arriving every week. While old model businesses fail faster, new models are scaling faster. Whoever heard of Netflix or Uber or Airbnb or Wayfair or Casper until, almost all at once, they were everywhere? Even strategy itself, the time-honored bedrock of modern business, once framed in decades (and if it wasn't it didn't really count as strategy), is now wisely revisited more frequently. In the corporate world, "change management" is now actually a discipline. Degrees and entire academic institutions are now devoted to change, and a $10 billion service industry is growing in support of it.

Change is clearly upon us as never before. The very idea of a technology-fueled "age of change" is so firmly rooted in today's zeitgeist that it is not enough to be comfortable with change, or even good at it, we need to become *really, really good at it*. Like, performance athlete good.

The serial killer of great companies

Here is a puzzling question: If we all know the pace of change is quickening, and we accept that the things we depend on—our livelihoods, the companies we work for, and valued institutions—must keep pace, not just to survive but to thrive, wouldn't it make sense to wholeheartedly embrace change? At the precise moment it is clear to us that the status quo isn't the smartest choice any longer, shouldn't we naturally say to ourselves, "I think I had better get moving to not get left behind." Well you would think so, and it would be completely rational, but that's just not the way we humans think and behave. Fundamentally, we just don't like change. So, in one way or another—either taking a visible and defiant stand against it, or just surreptitiously resisting it—we simply avoid *doing it* in favor of keeping things as they are, come what may.

It's a human nature thing. If only we didn't hang on so tightly to what we know and are comfortable with, believing it will last forever. If only we didn't see change as some nefarious interloper come to ruin everything (to the point, new model businesses these days are referred to as "disruptors"). If only we could position change in our minds as *good* and not *bad*, embracing it as a force for gain well worth some degree of pain. If only we could see the need for change sooner, and sooner accept that nothing is immune from it. Wouldn't we all be a little or even a lot better off? The answer is yes. Yes, we would. Change in fact *is* a good thing, and resistance to it is almost always futile (Darwin and his theory of survival of the fittest comes to mind as an instructive primer in this regard). Instead, we watch perfectly good businesses and their leaders actively choose the status quo and ride it off a cliff.

What makes this tragic is that it doesn't need to be this way. Sears, the company that gave my dad a gold watch on his twenty-fifth anniversary, and was at one time 1 percent of the GDP of the U.S. economy, did not need to fail. Organized religions, in my case the Catholic Church I grew up with, do not need to continue their acceleration into irrelevance and antiquity. Individuals needn't continue their angst-filled journeys into professional obsolescence. Rather, the status quo itself should be tacked on a wall as the poster example of what is out of date.

Meanwhile, there are companies accepting the need to change, getting on with thoughtful evolution, and continuing to grow and prosper. Nike is one. Apple continues to be one, as do McDonald's and Starbucks. Sadly, though, these are the exceptions and not the rule. How many long-standing companies have slipped below the water line, or are flirting with it? It is a very long list getting longer. Instead of figuring out how to adapt and evolve, becoming as good at change as any other vitally important competency, many companies instead lurch from crisis to crisis. Of the companies listed on the Fortune 500 in 1955, only sixty remain today.

The idea of *what once was great is now great again* seems to have gone out of favor. Now, *what once was great* is regularly being replaced by *what's new*. Blockbuster was replaced by Netflix and Hulu, it didn't become them. Even though it invented the digital camera, Kodak was replaced by digital photography; it did not become the iPhone and Instagram. Taxi cabs are being replaced by Uber and Lyft, rather than evolving to eliminate the need for disruptors in the first place. Furniture stores are being replaced by Wayfair, and Amazon is doing its best to replace every retailer in the western hemisphere. It's completely unnecessary. Continually creating a better version of themselves should not have been a remote possibility for these companies, but a mandate. Who better to create the better version of a company than the company itself?

Jim Collins, a thinker and author I admire, wrote about getting from good to great, and about why great companies fail. What I've spent the last fifteen years working to understand is how companies can continue to be great *without failing*—or at least without needless crises, extended runs of underperformance and irrelevance, and the inevitable dramatic intervention or farewell liquidation. Otherwise *there is a serial killer of companies on the loose—the status quo*—and it is coming for every slow-moving and change-resistant organization on the planet.

There are rules to this game and it's wise to know them

I eventually realized that my relationship with change and the status quo was different from most. What I gathered—first from my family, then through industrial design school (learning what would now be referred to as "design thinking"), and finally, through consecutive career reinventions leading to *Reinventionist*—is that life gets easier and more rewarding once you understand the rules:

Change is hard. Irrelevance is harder.

Change is not risk, it is opportunity. Today the greater risk lies in staying put.

Change before you have to—always—and understand that you always have a choice. The only catch is that if you don't exercise it, choices will be made for you.

Change comes with roadblocks. There will always be something in your way, always something pushing hard against you. In this regard, speed is an ally to overcome these barriers and momentum helps crash through all that stands in your way.

Change does take a village.

And, lastly:

The surest way to stay true to who you are—company or brand or even individual—is to reinvent, so as to continually become the most powerful and relevant version of yourself.

This last point is the heart of my thesis.

Looking back, now with the kind of daybreak clarity that only hindsight brings, I realize that change wasn't a force taking me further from what I knew, further and further into the unknown, as we all fear it will. Instead it brought me back again and again to who I truly am. As I have worked closely with leadership of dozens of companies, helping to get them on a path back to growth and relevance, it has been proven in the marketplace, too. At the heart of it all is a powerful yet counterintuitive idea: the surest way for any organization to become its truest and best "self" is to get really good at reinventing itself.

Right there within the word "reinvention" is this central idea embodied, the *re* being a continual return to the original *invention* so it can be remade. The opposite of throwing everything out and starting again. The opposite of becoming something else entirely. Instead, a deep understanding and riff off the original idea. Updating and adapting it to the present moment and possibilities. Always sharpening its focus while striving to innovate and make it better. Truly grasping that any kind of "FROM/TO" journey should not be a *big change moment,* but a fluid state of continually evolving and improving toward an outcome. Becoming a Reinventionist is to achieve this higher-level state.

3

The five principles of the Reinventionist Mindset

H ERE'S A SHOCKER:

It's not enough to *know*. We must *do*.

Let's appreciate what reinvention is, and understand its great power and promise of renewal. More importantly though, let's learn how to put together the *knowing* and *doing* parts so we can make change possible. This has been my own personal and professional journey.

Although not consciously at first, in reinvention after reinvention, I began taking note of what was working—ways of doing things that would galvanize a team or cause results to come faster. These would surface as instinctive adjustments to the sequence of actions my team and I would take to successfully bring about change (what would eventually become a playbook of reinvention), together with adjustments to how we would behave throughout. I began to think of the *what* and *how* as two halves of a complete whole. First, an end-to-end *method*, the step-by-step way to go about uncovering insights, choosing strategy, aligning organizational focus, resetting the value proposition, reshaping customer experience, and activating it inside and in the market (what I will cover in chapter twenty-three). And second, a complementary *mindset*, a set of principles that would encourage the right behaviors along the way. This procedural and behavioral combination proved to be a powerful one-two punch. The more we tinkered and honed, the more we enabled and empowered our clients—the companies we partnered with to reinvent—the sooner they were on their way to successful outcomes.

I first wrote the Reinventionist Mindset down when reflecting on the reinventions of Duane Reade and Old Navy. Each engagement was hugely successful (as measured by performance improvement, strength of strategic position, customer love, and, ultimately, the overall value of the enterprise) and both were what I now consider the beta test of the method and mindset my team and I still practice a decade and a half later. I will share the method at the end of the book, but here now—with input from my colleagues at Jackman Reinvents, who have helped me simplify and sharpen these over the years—are the five very human principles of the Reinventionist Mindset:

Seek Insight Everywhere. We humans are naturally curious, so flex that muscle to look beyond what's obvious. Dig deep. Find the nuggets within your own story that sharpen your view of who you are and what is uniquely possible. Understand what others are doing within your category, but look to other categories for inspiration. The world around you is constantly changing so attune your ear to the faint signals of what is coming. Above all, be deeply curious about human nature and what truly motivates us, as this is the golden key to value creation.

Embrace Uncertainty. We humans have natural instincts. Learn to use and trust yours. Balance facts with feelings, as they are of equal value. Use facts to inform hunches, and then lean in to them rather than rationalize your way back to the status quo. Find the courage to move while you prove, and never be daunted by small failures.

Create the Future Now. We humans are built for the future, yet if we're not careful we will be defined by and held to our past. Never let what's behind you hold you back from the future you decide upon. And never wait. Move forward at a pace. Balance getting it right with getting on with it. The future isn't some far-off place: it arrives daily, so own it.

Obsess the Outcome. We humans will readily move toward a place we can picture in our minds and get excited about. At the outset of any transformative journey, always paint a picture of the outcome you intend to achieve—in words and images as well as numbers, altogether a compelling story of where you are going and why. Hold it up for all to see, and then be relentless in your pursuit of it.

Make Momentum Together. We humans tend to support that which we help to create, so collaborate and watch how input makes things stronger—ideas, strategies, and teams—*and* how full buy-in sparks energy and momentum. You want momentum on your side as it becomes an unstoppable force, able to crash through any and all barriers in your way.

Each of these principles is rooted in human nature, gathered from many years of working with, and learning from, people engaged in change. With strong leaders in a difficult spot in their careers. With entire communities under extreme pressure, when time and money were running out. With humans faced with the challenge of change and hard choices. Through it all, it was human nature that surfaced to either overcome these challenges or succumb and be defeated by them. In every situation, no matter how grave, there was always a way forward. There was always a choice. And, it was always human nature that made the call, one way or another.

Looking back, it wasn't circumstances or even strategy that made the difference between success and failure, *it was people*. I made a point of digging deep into what makes us all tick when change is upon us. What excites us. What scares us. What gives us hope, comfort, and confidence. What causes us to passionately move ahead, or crumples us to our knees. Through multiple business reinventions—over forty companies and counting— these five principles emerged. They are deceptively simple, almost to the point of being easily dismissed. But to do so would be to miss what makes them so effective and powerful, individually and in combination. They are as simple as common sense. They go right to the heart of why change slows us to a crawl, or veers us off course to a fiery crash. Instead, they keep us on the road accelerating into the curve. They are the game changers of change itself.

In the chapters that follow I will demonstrate why these principles work. But let's prove and move together. *I* will share each principle followed by the real-life stories that reveal its origins and what makes it essential, if *you* will think about how to relate to and apply them to your own situation. Deal? My intention is to persuade you to love change as I do. To learn the "human how," as different from the way change typically comes about in the corporate world (as I will describe in the next chapter, the Loblaw story). Ultimately, to *become a Reinventionist*. Although you and I have traveled different paths to get to this moment, let there be no doubt the business world today needs more of us.

4

From darkness to light (and from WTF to AHA)

The Loblaw story

ROM A TOP-FLOOR meeting room window, across the long view of a windswept cornfield and the jutting remains of last season's crop, I could feel the warmth of the early sun and hear the automated window shutters racing to blunt its glare. Viewed from the nearby toll freeway, the new Loblaw Companies' headquarters—a shiny glass, metal, and concrete cube on the outskirts of Toronto—would have appeared like the Star Trek *Enterprise*, snared by an insistent tractor beam drawing it toward its fate. It was the fall of 2006, and I had been the Executive Vice President of Marketing for Canada's largest retailer for a year and a half. I was feeling the pull of something equally insistent and threatening, as the guy who had hired me had exited the building precipitously, and all hell was breaking loose.

Loblaw was a legendary Canadian supermarket company with a long history of game-changing innovation—from cutting-edge store designs to powerhouse private brands such as President's Choice—that had moved it from the brink of bankruptcy in the early seventies to outsized dominance by the early nineties. In the ensuing decades it could seemingly do no wrong, and its lofty stock price was a daily reminder of its strength in not only food and home goods, but affordable fashion and financial services. Were it not for the arrival of a gentleman from Arkansas named Sam Walton, who had a different idea of what the Canadian retail landscape should look like, Loblaw's strong run could have continued uninterrupted.

In 1994, Walmart landed in Canada with a bang, acquiring the national Woolco chain from the F. W. Woolworth Company, bringing with it its low-cost operating ethos, relentless focus on price, and centralized buying power. In an instant it was a national player, efficient in every regard and strong enough to singlehandedly reset the "price floor," the price Canadians could expect to pay for household goods. When Walmart aggressively expanded their supercenter store format, adding groceries to increase the frequency with which shoppers would visit, they directly took on the grocery market leader Loblaw. Consumer prices plummeted. Profit margins eroded. Market share shifted. For the first time since achieving market dominance, Loblaw had a true national competitor and its arrival exposed a soft underbelly.

Loblaw was built as a roll-up of regional chains, each one left to operate with its own playbooks, buying practices, and banners. The magic of this formula was a collection of regionally strong and familiar store chains tailored to local expectations, and behind the scenes a financial roll-up reflecting control of the lion's share of food sales across the country. There was a lot to admire about Loblaw, including a deep expertise in private brands and its successful strategy of owning its own real estate. Yet, the sum of Loblaw parts did not add up to a highly efficient national whole, from its supply chain to the cost of goods sold. Now faced with head-to-head competition of a very different kind, it was vulnerable.

By the time John Lederer took the helm of Loblaw as President, in November of 2000, a battle for dominance was raging and the most populous province of Ontario was ground zero. As Walmart aggressively added more stores in the center of the country, Loblaw stores got bigger and bigger— with more footage added for general merchandise and apparel—while prices went lower and lower. It was a market-by-market street fight and as a consultant to Loblaw I was kept busy working with leadership to retool store formats, sharpen communications, amplify private brands, and build a new brand called Joe Fresh—with the brilliant Joe Mimran at the helm designing a line of stylish and affordable clothing—to blunt Walmart's low-price apparel offering. We all fought the good fight, but it could not make up for the fact that the company was structurally disadvantaged. It became clear that complete centralization, from supply chain and merchandising/marketing functions to operating structure, would be necessary. It was at that point that I was offered a newly created executive position, the first-ever national Marketing Leader. With a mix of excitement and anxiety, I sold my company, left consulting, and joined Loblaw.

But wait. How the heck did that wild-haired kid in 1970s Windsor get to be an executive at one of Canada's largest corporations?

Misfits, mentors, and magic makers

"Joe has some talent. Too bad he's a yahoo."

That comment, a verbatim quote from a grade ten report card, pretty much sums up my high school years. While peers studied and excelled academically, I channeled my energy into other so-called extracurricular pursuits. Guitar playing. Tennis. Card games. Forest running (the rural version of what would now be called parkour). Drawing. A constant rearranging of the contents of my parents' home. Anything and everything but schoolwork. By age sixteen, I had a business card and was making furniture in my Dad's garage. I lived for the weekends when my siblings returned home and I could soak up every detail of their worlds. At least until I could design and build my own.

As a design school student, I was blessed to have a recent immigrant to Canada as a professor. Alexander Manu, a creative prodigy from Romania, had both talent and a huge disdain for the visual landscape of his newfound home ("Design doesn't exist here"). He took a ragtag bunch of young adults and proceeded to completely blow our minds with his views on everything from how to dress ("Mostly khaki, and if that is in the laundry wear black"), what to read ("Throw away your stupid magazines. Read *Abitare*," even though that particular design and architectural magazine was entirely in Italian), the way one should eat ("Never use two hands when you eat chicken wings. You always want one hand clean and free to point at things you don't like"), and even the name we should greet one another with ("Hello Sergei," to which I would reply, "Hello Sergei"). This last bit done in jest of course, yet I suspect with a not-so-subtle point: you are no longer who you once were. My design school years under Manu were nothing less than an intensive and thorough reprogramming of my aesthetic and cultural sensibilities. I was taught to tear things apart and put them back together in more thoughtful ways. I experimented. I failed. I tried again. Ultimately, I experienced the rush of defining a clear outcome, designing to it, and then seeing it through to realization.

My first big job in the creative industry, beyond freelancing and a stint with a start-up design firm, was with the internationally acclaimed designer Don Watt. What made Watt a respected innovator was how he linked creative solutions with business objectives, going after the boldest and simplest design solution to deliver the greatest sales impact. Watt is credited with inventing "photo realism," a creative tactic now common today, where a glass jar of unappetizing dehydrated coffee crystals from Nestlé was magically transformed into the gorgeously rich coffee beans pictured on the label. The approach completely changed the quality perception of the product and the price consumers were willing to pay, and sales went through the roof. While Manu gave me a critical eye and an acute design sensibility, Watt changed what I could do with it.

When I left The Watt Group to start the creative consultancy Perennial with founding partner Cam Whitworth, a close design school friend and creative powerhouse, we had no idea it would become one of Canada's largest and most successful design and branding firms. As President for sixteen years, it was my job to oversee a team servicing some of North America's most well-known brands and retailers. Our largest client? Loblaw Companies.

Full circle

So here I was, now an executive at Loblaw after a decade and a half of being a consultant for the company on everything from brand strategy and store design to retail communications. In less than the time it took to finish a cup of coffee, I accepted Loblaw President Lederer's job offer, sold my business to my partners, and effectively blew up my quite comfortable professional life to go on an adventure into corporate leadership and the unknown. But I knew Lederer well, by this time considering him a friend and mentor, and every bit of what followed was exactly what I hoped it would be. Until, of course, the day he unexpectedly left the company and the world went to heck in a handbasket.

While the restructuring of the company under Lederer was well underway, it had not gone as planned. Differing views of what came next caused Lederer and the company to part ways, and he relinquished his role as President; that's when the real craziness began. A triumvirate of new leaders was appointed. Big consulting firms were brought in and their teams camped out in every corner of the business. Wave upon wave of employees were let go, beginning at the top and working downward and deeper (I can still see in my mind's eye team members heading into meeting rooms with their windows papered over, exiting minutes later with bewildered and tearful gazes). It seemed that every day there was another newspaper headline referring to the steady stream of top-ranking executive departures and perceived transformational missteps. And all of it was apparently no surprise. As I would hear from those who had experienced these things in other big companies, this was what corporate restructuring looked and felt like.

Now that Lederer was gone, my first instinct was to follow him out the door along with other executives closest to him. But I loved the company, in some ways having grown up with it, and I hadn't accomplished what I had joined it to do, namely refresh the flagship brand President's Choice, launch the apparel brand Joe Fresh, and build a national marketing capability. Most of all, here was a rare chance to experience firsthand a massive corporate transformation *from the inside*. I simply couldn't pass it up. When I was asked to stay on, I agreed.

What came next was a surprising invitation to join the Restructuring Committee, a small inner circle of executives who would meet weekly to oversee the company's transformation. Wow. Only my schooling in industrial design was remotely connected to breaking a giant company down to its bolts and building it back up again, and that was a stretch. But, as was explained to me, leadership felt I would add a valuable perspective and my history and relationships within the company would be helpful. I was about to learn firsthand that restructuring big companies is a messy business, and if you are management it's better to be liked than demonized.

Tension, uncertainty, and even outrage. These were the daily norms at Loblaw in those difficult days, the hallways buzzing daily with fresh grievances and whispers of who was next to go. It seemed that pretty much everything that had previously been held up as important was being systematically attacked, and symbols of merciless change could be seen everywhere. A feature of the new office, a five-story totem memorializing the ideals and values of the company—emblazoned with words like "respect," "passion," "insight," "community," and "diversity," the result of an internal employee poll taken in the early stages of new office planning—had been stripped in the dark of night and replaced with just three new ones: "Simplify, Innovate, and Grow." There could be no more dramatic break from the past than this gesture, the equivalent of smashing statues of previous leaders and leaving the rubble to make a point. And right there, looking up at that altered totem, came my WTF moment. Is this really the way change happens in the corporate world?

A moment of clarity followed by an exit

I've since studied companies and their transformations, and learned they share a common dynamic: in crisis they are divergent, where everything is in a state of chaos and coming apart, until they are convergent again, where everyone eventually aligns and settles into the new way forward. For Loblaw, that convergent moment was engineered to take place in the form of a leadership rally in the late fall of 2006, nearly a year and a half after my joining and a few months after Lederer's departure. Ideally, the initial shock has passed, a common sense of purpose is established, and everyone rallies around new leadership and gets on with it. Ideally.

Two hundred of the top executives gathered in a large room that day—an outsized employee training facility on the main floor of Loblaw headquarters—to hear leadership articulate their vision for the future of the company. The vibe was intensely anxious, and in the front-row seats was the eleven-person Executive Vice President team. Behind us were the Senior Vice Presidents, Vice Presidents, and Directors of the company, collectively our direct reports and theirs. Those of us in the front row that day—choosing to remain, or possibly waiting our turn to be taken out—shared a deep sense of responsibility, and the eyes of those gathered behind us boring into the backs of our heads. Simultaneously, we felt like survivors and traitors, as those who experience restructuring often do. The rally was more than a key meeting, it was a moment of truth, and everyone in the room that day knew it. Beyond answering the obvious question of where the company was going, top leadership knew they had to address the one question on everyone's mind: *When will the chaos end?* In exchange for the answer, what leadership hoped in turn to hear was a unanimous, "I am in." While the future could possibly be bright again—and I was doing my level best to be objective just like everyone else—it would be difficult for me to overcome so many perceived wrongs to even consider taking part in any future right.

The meeting ended with everyone presumably making up his or her own mind. While much was said with a lot of bravado, the result was less than full endorsement and more wait and see. I left the room with just one question on my mind:

> **Does corporate change really need to be this ugly
> and this demoralizing?**

Apparently, "yes" was the dumbfounding answer.

While it was clear Loblaw required substantial change for good reason, and it was in a hurry because it needed to be, it was the way in which the change was orchestrated that I could not get over. I had no prior corporate experience to compare it to and therefore didn't really know. But anyone could see this was messed up; this is not a critique particular to Loblaw, this is the way corporate restructuring often unfolds. And that was the AHA moment.

I made two decisions that day:

1   No, I wouldn't stay.
2   I am going to figure out how to do change better.

Strangely, the most difficult of professional moments turned out to be the defining one of my career, setting me on the path to becoming a Reinventionist.

A few months later, in the early spring of 2007, I was asked to leave and moved on with the rest, taking care to transition out over several months to avoid putting my team in an even tougher spot. My colleague, Paul Clark, Senior Vice President of Marketing, and my right hand through two-plus years, kept everyone focused and moving forward until his own exit a few months later. As I walked out the door of the office at 1 President's Choice Circle for the last time, into a setting sun casting long shadows on the building behind me, I had one final thought: *Wherever I go, whatever I do, I will never instigate or manage change in the way I experienced it here.*

A first glimpse of the human how

My time at Loblaw challenged me beyond anything I had experienced professionally up to that point. Having never previously been a corporate executive, I had fully expected that change would be hard. I wasn't prepared for brutal. Yet, as strange as it may sound, I am completely appreciative of every bit of it, and deeply grateful to those who gave me opportunity after opportunity to continue to stretch, grow, and add value.

Public company experience and retail exec boot camp? Check.

Learning to understand and operate within large company culture? Check.

Shaping strategy tied back to a P&L, which I co-owned with my peers, and then learning how difficult it really is to implement? Check.

Understanding what transformational change looks and truly feels like on the inside? Triple-check.

What I learned through this experience was that any kind of substantial corporate change will always be difficult—as difficult as the loss of colleagues and the fear of losing livelihoods can be—and that many of those impacted will not be happy with the decisions made. This is the hard reality of change. Yet within all the angst and turmoil that was Loblaw, an insight emerged that would stay with me. Large companies are not faceless and inanimate objects, as we often perceive them to be. Rather, they are particularly and profoundly *human*. It would follow then that how we go about changing them must be thought of and brought about in *human terms*. Otherwise, they come apart at the seams and stay that way for a very long time. Rare for a consultant, I had the immersive and visceral opportunity to learn there is a right and a wrong way to go about making big change. The right way asks for acknowledgment and acceptance that transformation is fundamentally *a human endeavor with a business consequence* and not *a business endeavor with a human consequence*. Said another way, get it right with people and therefore get it right for the business. Change is a collaborative sport. Whether people stay or move on, the more you work with them and bring them along on the journey the faster you'll get through it and back to winning. Or, you can ham-fistedly make change with little explanation or consideration; you can simply rule it into being and expect everyone to pick up the pieces. Guess what? They won't.

The choice is ours to make, and it turns out to be binary. One way will yield lingering consequences—consequences like cultural toxicity, chronic underperformance, and lost opportunity. The better way will take us to early alignment, commitment, and momentum, as I will demonstrate in the chapters that follow. This better way is innately human, upping the odds of a successful outcome. The first inkling of it came to me during my time at Loblaw. Within that dark moment and place was a bright and hopeful sliver of light: when change is upon us, as it will be more frequently, the method and mindset of how we go about it is *everything*.

PART TWO

THE HUMAN HOW

or

The five principles of the Reinventionist Mindset explained, with behind-the-scenes stories illustrating how to use them (and what happens if you don't)

5

First Mindset Principle

Seek Insight Everywhere

L ET'S BEGIN THE journey to Reinventionist with a definition of what it is to be one:

Reinventionist. *A bold, magnetic doer with the mindset to make transformative change possible; a master of the art and science of reinvention; an expert at identifying and actioning insights to create value.*

This is what a Reinventionist is and does. In large part becoming one will call on you to further develop your natural abilities to identify insights. They are that important. The *Merriam-Webster Dictionary* defines "insight" as:

1   **the power or act of seeing into a situation;**
2   **the act or result of apprehending the inner nature of things or of seeing intuitively.**

Every reinvention is a FROM/TO journey. Seeing intuitively what is happening *within and around* a business is important; the business world generally gets this, seeking out market and competitive insights. More to the point though, what is happening with *people* within and around a business—those working in it, those engaged with it as customers, or those collectively shaping trends around it through their decisions every day— is essential. You cannot reinvent without meaningful human insights. So much so that I would say it this way:

No human insights, no strategy.
No strategy, no successful FROM/TO.
No FROM/TO, no extraordinary value creation.

As you will see in the stories that follow, a human insight is worth its weight in gold because it does one thing: it reveals how to unlock new ways to create value.

With that in mind, here's the definition of "insight" I work with:

> **A fundamental human truth one can uncover and action to create value.**

It's similar territory to the dictionary definition, but mine is squarely focused on humans and what motivates them, then pitched toward action. If you cannot *do* something with an insight, it actually isn't one.

The first principle of the Reinventionist Mindset is *Seek Insight Everywhere* and there are multiple places to look. Here are six:

Start with your customer. What do they care about? No, not the obvious stuff. What do they *really care about*, and what are they really buying from you beyond products or services? Beyond the functional and into the emotional. Is it confidence? Happiness? Fulfillment? There is no downside to investing into a deep understanding of what your customers really value beyond the functional, and how one group of customers with like-minded values and motivations behaves differently from another. Not only will doing so be foundational to your business and brand strategies, it will help you determine exactly *for whom* you are designing your customer experience and proposition. If you don't have that sharp focus and clarity, you are guessing, and Reinventionists don't guess.

Look within your company. This is where the concept of DNA, or the code of what makes each of us who we are as individuals, comes into play for companies of all kinds. It makes sense because businesses are, after all, human constructs; people created them based upon their own values and the opportunities they saw at the outset. It is essential for you to know your company's code.

Hertz was hardwired by its founders to be about the *best cars, fast and easy.* When we began its reinvention this original DNA was still there, although hiding in plain sight. When we compared these DNA strands with what research revealed customers really cared about, it turned out to be a perfect match. Hertz had simply drifted away from what had been true all along, or at least what was supposed to be true. Getting back to it—making it central and celebrating it again—reenergized the business, and it was this *reinvention of the original invention* that returned Hertz to growth. Such is the power of insights, and DNA is a particularly useful type.

Look within your category. What are people excited about within your category these days? Are there new players, the so-called disruptors, doing things in exciting new ways? Are your old rivals experimenting with innovations you can learn from? What's causing the change? When I worked on Duane Reade, I learned from what the Boots drugstore chain was doing in the U.K., and what Shoppers Drug Mart was doing at home in Canada. Not just *what* they were doing but *why*. The more drugstores became convenient, daily "life-in-a-box" partners, the more customers rewarded them with spending and loyalty, as this resonated with the hectic nature of modern life. In this regard there could be no more extreme circumstance than life in New York City, and the insights gathered by digging deep into those examples unlocked a different and more expansive view of what was possible. Sushi in a drugstore? Not as crazy as it first sounded.

Look outside your category. Get inspired by what others are doing well beyond your realm. If you attend conferences, attend some that have little or nothing to do with your business. Think about how innovation from without can be applied within, and why it is resonating with people in the first place. Consider what you come into contact with in your personal life that's new and exciting. Could it somehow be applied? For example, the birth of Uber did more to change consumer expectations of what "easy" looks like within the banking sector than anything initially done by the banks; why can't banking (or fill-in-the-blank category) be this easy? There is a high likelihood of innovation traveling from one category to another, so why not be the first to consider doing it?

Look at what's happening in the world. What are people excited about around the globe that can help you think differently about the future? What are the trends—but more importantly the early indicators of *future trends*—that show you where the world is going? Read. Travel. Talk with people about what excites them these days. Notice and pay attention to what is happening around you, the curious things that ping and seem to want to tell you something. These are insights that can and will help you reinvent. When asked why he was such a gifted hockey player, fellow Canadian Wayne Gretzky replied: "I skate to where the puck is going to be, not to where it has been."

Look within. Lastly, dig deep for insights within yourself. What are you caring about these days? What excites you or even scares you? Becoming a skilled digger for insights starts with how well you are tuned in to *you* and your own experience, and it can evolve from there into a finely tuned radar for what lies beyond. Insights are the live ammunition of strategy.

Do strategy better

In June of 2008, at the Retail Council of Canada's annual leadership conference in Toronto, I gave a keynote speech to about 800 of the country's top retail leaders. My message was intended to be provocative and a call to action: the conventional way of shaping strategy, as practiced by business leaders and management consultants for generations, is deeply lacking and out of sync with the times. Unusual for a keynote, it was a fairly aggressive takedown of the traditional way of developing business strategy, long viewed as unassailable in its approach. The thesis I unpacked that day was this: The old way of doing strategy is flawed because it settles for facts over insights. It's flawed because too few are involved in shaping it. It's flawed because the most fundamental pieces are not tied together. It's flawed because it does not conceptualize the outcome. Finally, it's flawed because it falls short of connecting with and motivating people to buy into it and make it happen. We must do it better.

The consensus reaction could be summed up as "Why is Joe telling us this? Things are fine as they are, and all that customer insight stuff seems a little squishy anyway."

Yes, it was. But only if you consider the human part of strategy development—from the human insights that unlock value creation to a more collaborative process that leads to full alignment and buy-in— as "squishy."

The speech itself preceded the recessionary reckoning of 2009, when the pace of change clicked into overdrive and the shortcomings of many businesses' strategies were laid bare. At the time I was deep into the simultaneous reinventions of Old Navy and Duane Reade, and I couldn't help but notice the more we humanized our strategic and financial intentions from front to back—made them about customers and what they cared most about, tied them to what the brand was about, and engaged everyone within the company differently—the more everyone got excited, bought in, and leaned in to change. We can and must do strategy better.

6

On your side

The Staples story

N 1986, TOM STEMBERG gleaned something that would both change his life and completely upend the retail status quo of his day. Rather than shopping for stationery and office supplies from small "mom and pop" outlets, overpaying and putting up with a limited selection, limited hours, and hit-or-miss service, he wondered why someone didn't gather it all up under one roof—pretty much everything a small business would need day to day—and make it more affordable and convenient. Today the market insight seems obvious, but back then it was breakthrough stuff: low prices, often the lowest in the market, together with one-stop-shop convenience. In one stroke of a pen, buying stationery and other office supplies became that easy, so much so that the very idea of "easy" was celebrated in the award-winning Staples advertising campaign "The Easy Button."

Like other so-called big-box retail concepts of that era, Staples hit the mark and scaled quickly, building store after store across the United States, eventually extending Stemberg's original concept around the world through acquisitions. It seemed Staples would never run out of new markets or new ways to pack more of what customers wanted into each store. If you were on that ride as an executive or shareholder, you remember it as incredibly exciting and very lucrative.

Then things changed, as they always do.

Imagine for a moment you are leading a thirty-something-year-old "category killer" with a stellar history of growth and success. Although you don't realize it at the time, your business has reached its peak and will never get any better than this. There is no more up to be had, only down. What first appears as more road ahead is instead the beginning of a steep and steady decline. But you don't know that yet. In that moment you feel invincible. The stores are busy. Your B2B sales are booming. Your customers are satisfied. And your clout with the big brands you carry is such that you pretty much dictate your terms. You are not just *in* the category; you *are* the category. Sure, there are a few direct competitors and some upstarts here and there, but none of them are as large as you and none near your gold standard of success. This is as good as it gets.

When exactly did it happen? When did the downturn in sales, a blip at the time, become a trend? When did customer satisfaction scores begin to soften and then slide? When did the interlopers start to take a little and then a little more? When did the national brands, partners for all these years, take a firmer stance in price negotiations and squeeze margins as theirs were once squeezed? And, when did the business go from "latest and greatest" to yesterday's idea, with media columns that once heaped praise now insultingly documenting your decline?

This is what the end of a successful era looks and feels like. These are the dynamics of a business left too long without reinvention. It's the end of the party and indeed it sucks, the penalty for stubbornly hanging onto the past. This was Staples only a few short years ago. Past its peak. Under pressure and slipping under water. A long, long way from easy.

Around this time, I called Staples to introduce myself and share a point of view. It went like this:

"You have a great business founded on a simple idea, and from what I can see that idea is still relevant and powerful. Possibly even more so today. Yet how it shows up is increasingly irrelevant, in particular the stores. Now is the time to reinvent so you can keep on thriving. But you don't have a lot of time to decide."

I recall the senior-most executives at the time being very generous with their time, attentive and curious. Yet the elephant in the room (or, as they say in Canada, the moose on the table) was that they were in the toughest of all situations, where the need for bold thinking and substantial intervention coincides with the least amount of room to maneuver and wherewithal to afford change. It's not a spot you wish to find yourself in.

In the end, we wished each other well, they thanked me for my time and perspective, and declined to engage. And that would likely have been that, but for a twist of fate.

In June 2017, Staples was acquired by Sycamore Partners, for $6.9 billion, and John Lederer, with whom I had collaborated previously, had joined Sycamore as Senior Advisor.

When the deal went down, the business media and retail pundits were aghast at the price paid for the company. Almost unanimously, the outcry was "Mistake!" *Bloomberg* coverage at the time noted: "It's a lot of money for a company in secular decline," and "This idea of selling office supplies from brick and mortar stores is not the wave of the future. Amazon, Walmart"—they with their aggressive pricing, direct delivery, buying clout, and customer reach—"are obviously getting into this business."

Now smart private equity partners, Stefan Kaluzny of Sycamore Partners clearly amongst them, do not like to guess. To determine the price they are willing to pay for a company, and, to the extent humanly possible, de-risk the transaction, they conduct "due diligence," the term used for deep, pre-deal analysis and scenario development that leads either to a bid or a pass. In the event of a bidding battle this information is returned to again and again, reworked and scoured for the confidence to pay just a little bit more to win the prize. It's an incredibly interesting, fact-based process that distills down into one primary thesis: how value will be created. This thesis lays out what to do, typically along these lines:

- Restructure debt and rework the balance sheet
- Drive process and other efficiencies
- Lower cost of goods sold (COGS) and take operating platform cost out
- Divest non-core assets
- Acquire synergistic assets

While there can be variation depending upon the asset and its situation, this is the time-honored playbook of private equity, and it has worked phenomenally since its inception in the early eighties (it was made notorious in the book *Barbarians at the Gate*, the story of KKR and its acquisition of RJR Nabisco).

Most notably in the playbook, however, is what is *not* there. Seldom will you hear *transform the customer experience and value proposition*, simply because the prospect of completely retooling a company—from business model to how it goes to market—stretches beyond the comfort zone of most private equity firms.

It makes sense. Why transform a business when what you might describe as "financial engineering" will deliver expected returns on your investment? Conventional thinking held that reinvention was something you did only when things went terribly wrong, and this is precisely what made the Staples deal such a risky bet in the eyes of so many. Most concluded that, to have a shot at truly winning again, the business would have to be almost completely retooled and reimagined. Considering the success rate of returning late-model retail "category killers" to growth (look no further than Toys"R"Us, Linens 'n Things, and Circuit City) the deal came with long odds. This was clearly a case where financial engineering *and* reinvention were Plan A, and the bet riding on that plan was nearly $7 billion.

So that's where we started.

Now, I'm an optimist by nature. I believe there are very few flagging businesses that cannot be returned to growth and relevance. Some would say that, over the course of my career, I've worked hard to prove that point, a typical refrain being "Joe, why the heck would you get involved with that #$&%*@! business?" Professionally, however, I am a realist, with a set of criteria that have helped me decide which so-called losers to put my team's weight behind—or which ones truly do deserve that billing. I haven't always gotten it right, so my criteria have evolved over time to these four main points:

☑ Company/brand with good DNA and "bones"
☑ Motivated ownership

☑ Talented leadership
☑ Collective willingness and wherewithal to make change, with a bias
   toward bold action

If I can tick these boxes—and it is worth pointing out that three of the four are human factors—then at least the foundational conditions for success exist. The next level of assessment involves market conditions, competitive dynamics, and customer trends, and these will all factor in at some point alongside a deeper understanding of what is possible. The insights I spoke of earlier. But to a Reinventionist, these first four are collectively the green light to proceed to the next step. It also helps if my team and I can get excited by the prospect.

For me personally there is nothing better than taking a once-great brand and returning it to greatness. It takes me back to my schooling as an industrial designer, where pulling things apart to rebuild them into a better form and function excited me. I love the intellectual and creative challenge of it all, and I feed off the pressure that accompanies the responsibilities of making substantive change (whether it be reinventing a category with an upstart player like Flow Water, or a massive, best-not-to-look-down $7 billion bet like Staples). That and it's usually a lot of fun.

Despite a going-in sense that Staples was there to be reinvented, it was a little daunting in light of other analogous situations that led to outright failure. Only Best Buy was a beacon of big-box transformation, and the story of its reinvention was still in its early chapters. Yet, on the positive side, Staples was a B2B company as much as a B2C retailer, so the stores would be only one aspect of a successful transformation. There was also something in the Staples origin story that stayed with me, beneath the obvious idea of "everything under one roof": Stemberg's insight that what entrepreneurs really needed was a trusted ally. Something told me that this mattered.

I knew Lederer well and was excited about the prospect of working with him again. We had developed the kind of trust and ease that comes with fighting past battles together. He is an inspiring guy and one heck of a transformational leader, and while he would not take the reins as CEO of Staples, he would nonetheless guide the ship and find the right talent in his role as Executive Chairman.

Prior to the acquisition, I had never met the new owner of Staples, Stefan Kaluzny, but his reputation for boldness preceded him. Since founding Sycamore with Peter Morrow in 2011, he had focused mostly on retail, much of it found on the "last call" distressed rack. The *Wall Street Journal* reported that Kaluzny's firm had made "hundreds of millions of dollars in the struggling retail sector by investing in brick and mortar chains" ("How One Investor Made a Fortune Picking Over the Retail Apocalypse," March 21, 2018), zagging when the rest of PE were zigging out of retail. Staples was most definitely a zag, effectively throwing a bird to conventional thinking. I couldn't help but admire that.

On August 15, 2017, in a high-floor office on 57th Street in New York overlooking the majesty of Central Park—what I would consider one of the greatest home-court-advantage environments in which to be interviewed—I sat down for lunch with Kaluzny and Lederer to get to know one another and chat all things Staples. On the elevator ride up, John was generous with his guidance: "Try not to blow it."

It took only a few minutes to see that Kaluzny's reputation was well deserved. I could see in him this intense intellectual curiosity and inclination toward boldness. Like John and me, his passion for retail was also evident. The prospect of working on Staples with the two of them was compelling. But as our conversation unfolded, I came to understand that beneath the singular brand Staples were multiple businesses and channels, each in need of a strategic overhaul. This gig would be exciting yet complicated.

On the elevator ride down, having left Kaluzny and Lederer to chat (and presumably determine whether I had blown it or not), I thought to myself, *I would love to work with these guys on this, but seat belts will be required.* Lederer called me that evening to say, "We are in if you are."

I was. So where to start?

As always, we started by seeking fresh insights. Where is the business today and why? What's changed? Where is the money going? What do we know about the origin story? Are there particular strands of DNA that will teach us something about what made the business different and special in the first place? I've learned that the past opens up a contextual way of seeing a business: not what it is at present, but what it has always been, and what employees at all levels believe it to be. The past has a way of magically revealing glimpses of the future, and that was the truth with Staples.

In Staples' case there were three strands of DNA, like bright red threads that wove through its history: "everything you need," "make it easy," and "on your side." Each of these could be seen as evergreen, as relevant tomorrow as they were yesterday. Who wouldn't want everything they could possibly need, made super easy, and all of it from a trusted ally? On closer inspection however, what had fallen out of favor wasn't the relevance of the core ideas the business was founded upon, but their manifestation. Rivals had caught on and caught up, and the world was simply different than it was in 1986. "Everything you need" was now available everywhere thanks to the internet; and "easy" had been completely redefined, now with entire businesses that didn't exist previously (Amazon) built on that very premise.

But this idea of "on your side," part of Stemberg's original idea of existing to help the entrepreneur succeed, *this* was an intriguing strand, one that would turn out to be a treasure chest filled with possibility. Back then it translated into a primary focus on business customers rather than consumers, and a functionally defined offering: all the *supplies* they would need.

But what could it mean in the gig economy of today, when start-ups, side hustles, and technology-enabled disruption were the norm?

A few things to consider:

1   By the year 2020, over 40 percent of the U.S. workforce would be considered entrepreneurial—either self-employed in a small business, engaged in some kind of side hustle to their main job, or part of the rapidly growing "contingent" (contractors and freelancers) workforce. This had more than doubled from the mid-eighties, and it meant that much of what would have historically been taken care of by their employers was now on their shoulders, from tax remittance and administration to sales and marketing.

2   What entrepreneurs of all kinds were seeking wasn't just supplies—it was thoughtful, more holistic solutions to their challenges. Interestingly, this was also true of so-called intrapreneurs, entrepreneurial-minded office managers and buyers within larger companies.

3   What everyone wanted more than anything else was to be part of a community of peers that would inspire and cause them to see their challenges in new and innovative ways, and to help them learn, grow, and be fulfilled.

4   Lastly, something in what we were seeing and hearing was resonating with the brand's third DNA strand: "On your side." Which big brands stood out for independent businesspeople as being truly on their side? While they may say it, the evidence shows that none of them truly were. Not the banks. Not the telcos. Not the technology firms. And, despite the fact that it was part of Stemberg's original thinking, not Staples, either. Here was not only valuable white space, but something closer to a true purpose. What had struck me instinctively as being important at the outset was now appearing in the data, and a way forward began to emerge: a community of entrepreneurs with a thirst for solutions, in need of a trusted partner.

To a strategist this stuff is pure gold, the kind of macro and micro insights you can hang a sharp and actionable strategy on. So that's what leadership did.

As I look back on it, within eighteen months of that first meeting with Lederer and Kaluzny, we had not only collaborated with leadership to land a strategy for the three Staples operating units—the North American B2B business (led by CEO Sandy Douglas), the Canadian retail business (led by CEO David Boone), and the U.S. retail business (led by CEO Mike Motz)—but we also had five new and exclusive Staples private brands on the way (with Joe Mimran of Club Monaco and Joe Fresh fame, providing product design); two brand-defining stores, each a bold manifestation of strategy and including an in-store speakers' forum, a workshare space, and an expanded services hub. All of it was a straight line back to the original insights we had uncovered. Better still, we had growing proof the strategy was working, with substantial upticks in traffic, customer engagement, and sales.

What to take from this story? Insights are the raw materials of building and rebuilding empires, the golden keys to reinventing every company. Without insights you are guessing, and smart people don't guess.

What *not* to do in the face of change

Whether it's just the numbers that show your business is running out of gas, or there is further hard evidence that indicates more than a tweak or two will be required for it to grow, the following question will naturally come to your mind at some point:

How do I get out of this?

At that moment you have four real choices:

1 **Double down**. Your first option is to essentially keep doing what you have been doing, only harder, with the hope that the performance will return and the outcome will be different. If indeed the world has changed around you, and you've come to terms with that, this is definitely not the wisest choice. As Einstein reputedly pointed out, doing the same things over and over and expecting different results is the very definition of insanity.

2 **Strategize**. This is the very seductive second option, as it feels so good and smart to choose it. Simply stated, you initiate an endless loop of analysis, meetings, consultants' reports, and planning that ultimately yields nothing. For a time it appears that the challenge is being taken seriously and attacked thoughtfully, but eventually this wears thin, and inaction only compounds the problem.

3 **Ostrich**. Ignore all warning signs and take no action with hopes that whatever threats are out there will go away. This third option is in a dead heat with double down as the most popular choice.

4 **Reinvent**. Your fourth option. Build a foundation of "facts and feelings," develop deep insights from it, and use it to reset your strategy. Then, in a thoughtful and human way, get everyone on board, and fully activate it internally and externally to ignite momentum and rapidly return to relevance and growth.

Of course, every option but reinvent, which involves facing the need for change and actually making it, isn't a serious alternative. Each is merely a way of kicking the can down the road, increasing your risk, and making the inevitable choice to reinvent that much more difficult and expensive.

7

Like water in the desert

The Flow story

EVERY YEAR SINCE 1986, first in the form of a small gathering of friends on Baker Beach in San Francisco, then drawing ever more people to Black Rock City, Nevada, an annually-imagined city of now more than 70,000 rises from the desert, pulses with life for seven days, and is then completely burned to the ground to vanish without a trace. Burning Man, a unique arts and community festival, famous for its transient works of art as well as the artists and builders who attend each year, was founded on ten principles. Individually, each principle—for example, radical self-reliance, radical self-expression, and communal effort—guides engagement for all those who attend. Altogether they provide a general outline for a transformative act of collaboration that celebrates life and the very human act of creation.

Leave no trace. In 2013, this central Burning Man principle was on the mind of Canadian entrepreneur Nicholas Reichenbach, a "Burner"—the name given to those who return to the festival each year—in search of his next act. Reichenbach had created and sold several tech companies, mostly in the gaming space, but had an itch to do something more profound. Surprisingly, that itch would be scratched by garbage.

In the desert, not far from the pristine Joshua Tree National Park, there is little save for rocks, sand, and some of the most resilient flora and fauna found anywhere. Certainly no supplies for building a temporary city to house tens of thousands of attendees. No stores filled with food to feed them. No water, the most precious of all commodities in the desert, to keep all those good people from dying of thirst. Absolutely everything is carried onto the site and consumed by humans, and everything else is destroyed by fire. Or, almost everything. Each year tons of plastic, mostly containing hundreds of thousands of gallons of water, are trucked to the site for sustenance and then trucked away along with other garbage destined for recycling or landfill. It was these water bottles that would be Reichenbach's epiphany. How could such a mindful and purposeful festival like Burning

Man tolerate plastic bottles? In the bright sun of Black Rock City, it was a glaring oversight and an entrepreneurial opportunity writ large.

Reichenbach had a history with water. His family owned a spring from a deep limestone aquifer in Mildmay, Ontario, Canada, with a natural alkalinity amongst the highest on the planet. Truly, it was special water, with a natural pH level matched only by Fiji brand (another unique water from a similar aquifer on the other side of the planet), and millions of gallons of it were free-flowing from the ground daily. Over the years many had approached his father with the idea of bottling the water in plastic. But on environmental principles he had refused. With this history on his mind as he watched the cleanup at Burning Man, an idea popped into Reichenbachs' head: Tetra Pak. The innovative packaging format—100 percent recyclable and made from 75 percent recycled paperboard, with minimal plastic—was gaining popularity for beverages such as coconut water and juices, and was already the go-to choice for a growing community of global environmentalists and the socially-conscious. Why not natural spring water?

In 2013, the world didn't need another packaged water. The $157 billion global market was growing fast and estimated to reach $280 billion by 2020. The category was crowded with thousands of brands and a proliferation of "skus," which perfectly illustrated the problem: the world was awash in single-serving packaged water, most of it filtered tap water and almost all of it in plastic. Indeed, water in plastic was becoming the way most of us hydrated, spurred on by near-universal access, convenient portability, and the general misconception that it was safer than municipal tap water. Only later, well after this massive market shift had taken hold, did we collectively begin to realize the extreme detrimental impact on our health (microplastic) as well as our environment (macro- and microplastic). Images of acres of post-consumption plastic, all of it made from non-renewable oil and all of it adding to the carbon catastrophe foisted on the planet by the combined oil and plastics industries, began to flood the media, becoming daily reminders of the consequences of our choices. So too it was in the patch of desert called Black Rock City.

But what if the problem could become part of the solution? What if our insatiable desire to consume water from a convenient carry-along package could actually eliminate the need for single-use plastic? What if our deep need to have brands say something about who we are, the very hallmark of consumerism, could be harnessed to good effect instead of bad?

I first met Reichenbach a few months after his return from his 2013 Burning Man experience. We were introduced by a mutual friend and restaurateur, Hanif Harji, who felt we had a lot in common and thought I might be helpful as Reichenbach and his partner Tammy Eckenswiller began turning vision into reality.

Within a year, Reichenbach had secured a strategic relationship with Tetra Pak. As timing would have it, they were keenly interested in the idea of bringing to market a premium quality water in their uniquely shaped "prisma" packaging format. He had also secured the rights to the trademark "Flow" for the water category in North America, along with the website domain flowwater.com. As someone who has done a lot of naming and trademark work over the years, I could not have imagined a better set of assets to work with. The long and expensive journey of building a brand from scratch in a crowded category would be somewhat easier with a short and meaningful brand name and telegraphic URL. On the strength of Reichenbach's vision and persuasiveness, I became one of the early investors in Flow Water and signed on as a Board member and advisor, excited by the opportunity to help reinvent the packaged water category and do some social good.

Let's pause for a moment and move to the reason I am sharing this story with you. Flow Water, as good as it all was—the product, the name, the potential to reduce plastic usage, the market white space, and Reichenbach himself—had almost ZERO chance of success, for a long list of reasons:

- No one had ever heard of the brand, including retailers who would be expected to stock it without guarantee it would sell. It also meant straining their relationships with bigger beverage players, those with much deeper pockets and clout, in order to make room for Flow in their stores.

- Relative to the industrial-filtered tap water sold in cheap plastic bottles, Flow would be pricey. The cost of goods alone, a key benchmark in ensuring sufficient profit is available for both brand and retailer, was prohibitively high, made higher in the early days when Flow was filled by "co-packers," a handful of companies equipped to fill Tetra Pak for brands without their own packaging facilities. As a result, Flow would be priced 25 percent higher than any other premium brand on the market.

- Then there were regulatory considerations. Across North America, local, state/provincial, and even federal laws governing the commercial use of spring water were in flux. Increasingly there was controversy and much coverage in the media, along the lines of whether packaging spring water into single-serve containers was an appropriate use of a precious natural resource. The risk of a potentially interrupted supply due to government regulation shifts would surely be an issue for anyone considering Flow as an investment.

- Adding to these concerns is what I would call *offering confusion*, the killer of more than a few promising new consumer products. Proof-of-concept testing showed Flow (in an early silver version of the prisma package it continues to be sold in, along with a first-cut graphic brand identity) was regularly mistaken for coconut water and other beverages commonly found in Tetra Pak. Therefore, it was regularly passed over at the shelf. The early "pathfinder" retailers were raising flags.

If all of the above were not enough, where would the money come from to build a brand with customers, social influencers, and the media? To get listed with retailers across North America? To tell the story in such a way as to make the relatively higher price point appear as outstanding value for money? The investment would easily be in the tens of millions of dollars, excluding the steep price tag of setting up a dedicated Tetra Pak packaging facility.

As a consumer products analyst wrote in a memo to Reichenbach during the first fundraising round (and here I am paraphrasing):

Considering the many factors, from an overcrowded and commoditized water market dominated by global brands and their national retail partners, to the high cost of goods in an unconventional packaging format combined with the high risk of governments further tightening restrictions on spring water sourcing, I can only recommend that you do not proceed with the venture. I can only advise investors to do the same.

This was not the reaction anyone was looking for, and one heck of a tough message to swallow. But for Reichenbach's conviction and relentless perseverance, it may have been the end of the story. Yet there was a silver lining to the analysis. Indeed, it was thoughtful and completely rational commentary, and it caused everyone involved to dig deeper into the white space in the market and what consumers cared most deeply about. The brand needed a core insight on which to build a strategy, and already there were clues as to what that might be. As Eckenswiller pointed out, wellness was becoming the new luxury and consumers were increasingly buying on *values* versus value and functional benefits alone. Most premium water was sold with a relatively unemotional origin story (for example, Evian from the French Alps, or Fiji from Fiji) or with a focus on functional benefits (Smartwater, with added minerals and electrolytes). None however were tapping into a richer emotional mindset.

As we dug further, we came to understand that *doing something good for yourself* and *doing something good for the planet* were, on a deeper level, dimensions of a much more powerful idea. What people were really seeking was mindfulness and positivity. A high-pH, natural spring water in an environment-friendly Tetra Pak was the perfect embodiment of this core insight. I can recall the strategy workshop when everyone involved realized what we had uncovered and articulated. This was the insight we would build the brand on. As Reichenbach is fond of saying, "BOOM!!!"

Once we knew exactly what we were selling and why, it became crystal clear how we should go about it. The brand, playing the role of the "hero" archetype in Reichenbach's view, would be all about *complete and mindful positivity*, with a strong tilt toward those at the forefront of the well-being movement: women. With ample proof points in terms of product purity (natural source) and functional differentiation (high pH, inherent mineral content, both with plenty of health and beauty benefits), and a dramatically lower carbon footprint (Tetra Pak of course, but also through a decision to offer direct home/office delivery in major cities using a fleet of electric vehicles), no other water company in the world would come close to Flow's positioning and offer. Further proof came as Flow was awarded "B Corp" status in the United States, a high standard for companies with category-leading social and environmental practices.

The insight was there. The product/market fit was there. The will was there. The need was great. The only thing missing was a precise ambition beyond *let's build a premium water brand with benefits*. We needed a tightly defined outcome that would help focus and rally "everything and everyone" toward it and provide a more compelling proposition to investors.

If you are familiar with the notion of setting a BHAG, or "big hairy audacious goal" (an idea first conceptualized in *Built to Last: Successful Habits of Visionary Companies* by Jim Collins and Jerry Porras), then you can see why we concluded that, to be successful, Flow needed one—the bigger and bolder the better. Not just for its value as a galvanizer of effort, but as a means of framing that effort and the substantial investment required relative to the size of the prize. Everyone involved had to believe that the heavy lift would yield something profound, socially as well as financially. So, Flow's BHAG became this:

> **Within five years, become the fastest-growing premium spring water in North America, reach $100 million in sales, and therefore displace 100 million+ single-use plastic containers.**

These accomplishments would be the foundation to the ultimate BHAG:

> **Become the world's leading wellness water.**

Frankly speaking, this was flat-out crazy talk, particularly given the analyst's comments. But it did get the blood (and water) flowing.

From pre-launch tests early in 2015, through a full brand launch later that year—now with a retooled brand identity, new package design, and insight-led brand positioning and message—Flow Water has become part of the lives of 20+ million customers. It's sold in over 20,000 locations across North America, including Whole Foods, Sprouts, and Earth Fare, its first natural foods supermarket account in the United States (thank you Frank Scorpiniti, Earth Fare's CEO, for seeing the opportunity and believing in the brand). Customer love is huge—just search #flowwater and see for yourself—and retailer support continues to be strong. Best of all, Flow is now the *fastest-growing premium spring water in North America*. Above Fiji, above Evian, above Smartwater, all of which are sold in plastic containers.

What to take away from this story? First, it pays to get really clear about the outcome you intend to achieve, your BHAG, and the position you wish to occupy when you are done, as I will talk more about in chapter fourteen. The more you can picture it the likelier you are to achieve it. But the central point here is how game changing the right insights can be. As with the parable of Reichenbach and water in the desert, if you look, sustaining insights are there for you.

8

Second Mindset Principle

Embrace Uncertainty

T HE DILEMMA IS THIS: what stands in the way of progress is uncertainty, and we humans do not like it. We prefer reliability and predictability. We like to know what's happening and what *will* happen. We like to know what we can count on. This being true, what do we naturally do? We choose to stay put. We choose comfort over risk. We choose the status quo. And that is when we get into trouble. The full truth is that whatever *we* decide is only half of the success equation. If the world around us has decided to go in a different direction than we have, or is moving faster than we are, it's game over. Sure, it may take a while to completely take us out. But at a minimum it will mean fighting headwinds until the full-blown storm arrives. So, we have a choice, as we almost always do: run from uncertainty or learn to embrace it. I can tell you which choice will ultimately make you happier.

In a commercial context, investing into the future state of a business will always come with uncertainty. As business leaders we only know definitively what has worked in the past; anything beyond that is essentially a thesis of what may or may not work. It is therefore hard to predict the return on investment with any certainty. Say whatever you like about the present way things are done—whether manufacturing a product, selling a service, turning out a store, or operating a particular business model—even when it is underperforming at least it is *known*. At least it has a track record. Change it and who knows what might happen.

What's really interesting here is that even *considering* a new way can be disruptive to a business. Change causes all sorts of things to come into question. For example, what if the new way works? Does that mean we have to write off the old way and spend a ton of money to get onto the new? Might the new way require different skills and put my job at risk? Or, what happens if the new way doesn't work? Will I be embarrassed, or worse, fired? Change of any kind in business operates at a very human and personal level. When you put all these questions together you get a "no change" wall that becomes difficult to climb. Yet, to prosper, we need to change again and again and keep doing it. In essence that means figuring out how to *Embrace Uncertainty*. So, let's go after this brick by brick until that wall—the one we create in our minds—disappears.

Let's start by flipping the argument on its head and examine the one thing we *can* actually count on. *There is only one true certainty and it is that things will change.* While seductively appealing, the status quo is not actually an option, at least not for long. I hope you know that. By not embracing uncertainty you are actually doing yourself harm. It may sound odd, but it is foundational to how we must think and behave. The first step to embracing uncertainty is freeing ourselves completely from the notion that things as they are will remain as they are.

When it comes to risk you need to ask yourself a simple question: Where is your greatest risk coming from? Is it ahead of you, where the unknown resides, or is it all around you, in the present? It's a strange thought at first; that by staying where you are increases your risk. But it's actually the way things work. Getting stuck in the status quo puts you more at risk than anything that may come in the future. At least by participating in the future you have a real shot at competing in it. If you choose not to, you don't.

The same thing goes for reputational risk. I have witnessed firsthand how necessary change is halted because leaders wish to minimize their own risk of failure. But let me ask you another question: Would you rather be faulted for trying new things, or faulted for presiding over the past until it failed you and everyone else involved? Left unchecked, uncertainty is a formidable enemy. Better to embrace it and make it an ally.

Here's what I suggest you do:

- **Honor your past—just don't stay within it.** Celebrate where you have been while continually figuring out a better version of it. Define the present as a way station you are passing through.

- **Take leaps.** Always be thoughtful, yet nonetheless take leaps that move you forward and open up new possibilities. What is the worst that can happen? Your business fails before you take the leap is what.

- **Develop the skills and attitude of an entrepreneur.** Be optimistic. Passionate. Future-oriented. Relentless. Flexible. Resourceful. These are now requisite to leading businesses of all kinds.

In the end, embracing uncertainty is a calculation, weighing the risk of staying where you are versus the risk of moving ahead into the unknown. Everyone thinks that changing things is dangerous, but the opposite is true. If you do the honest math you will conclude as I have that the future is where you will actually be safest and most successful.

Staying uncomfortable

It's late 2016 and I'm on one of the top floors of a downtown bank tower in Toronto, enjoying a luncheon with a bunch of delightful high-schoolers. The room is buzzing, and I am happily learning about the Junior Achievement organization and the inspiring work they do with young people. It's a treat to hear students' ideas and sense their enthusiasm, and it takes me back to my first attempt at building a business when I was sixteen, a furniture company called Green Lane Pine I set up in my Dad's workshop. The business didn't last but my love of entrepreneurialism did, and here I was with a group of kids similarly bitten by the bug. My task on this sunny afternoon was to share some career advice that would help these kids on their way.

In some ways I would have liked to have been the guy on stage that day saying the expected things, like pick a lane and get a good education that will set you up for life (you should, at least to see where it leads). Consider life itself the best education you can possibly receive (it is). Or, choose a linear path and stick with it. I definitely couldn't share that bit, as my path wasn't even close to linear, and it led to a job I made up completely.

Every time I wished to advance in my career, to keep growing into the next thing that had captured my imagination, I firmly planted one foot in what I had learned and threw the other one as far forward into the unknown as I possibly could. In every one of those moments—some of them whoppers, like jumping from designer to strategist without a formal education in strategy, or from design firm President to Senior Marketing Leader without ever having held a marketing job—I had a sense of how I could add value, and certainly what I wanted to learn. Each time I was in over my head, and each time it was either sink or swim. I reflect on it sometimes and shake my head. Was it curiosity that caused me to make what were in hindsight very bold decisions? I like to think so. Ambition? Yes, more than a little. Naivete? Yep, most definitely. I remember a remark one of my closest friends and early business partners, Cam Whitworth, who, when we had set out together to build a design firm after college, said half-jokingly, "We are probably too stupid to know we can't do this." Such is the power of naivete.

I shared a bit of this journey with the students that day and then got to the point. The best career advice I can offer you is essentially the same advice I give to the leaders of companies I work with:

Stay uncomfortable.

9

Hold up,
it's working

The Vitamin
Shoppe story

N THE EARLY winter of 2017, Colin Watts, then CEO of The Vitamin Shoppe, took the stage at the annual NRF conference, America's leading retailer symposium, to deliver a much-anticipated presentation on reinvention. It was a packed house for many reasons, not the least of which was a softening share price and intense media scrutiny of his business.

The data Watts shared was more than encouraging. It was mostly centered on the bold reimagination of a store in East Rutherford, New Jersey, which had been renovated and then relaunched in September of 2016. This was the fullest expression yet of the strategy Watts and his leadership team, with my team's support, had put in place some months prior. A new store model was a vitally important plank of what would be a spectacular turnaround story, and with every proof point shared the audience could see success coming into view. The room was buzzing afterwards, and attendees from other legacy retail businesses were both impressed and inspired.

The Vitamin Shoppe was yet another retail chain left too long without a rethink, and as a result its stock price was getting hammered. When it came to which stick to beat it with, the analyst community had options. Declining same-store sales? Yes, a constant. Market share loss? Yep, that too. Competitive intensity? Definitely. Mass and drugstore players continued their insurgence into vitamins and supplements, once the exclusive domain of the specialty stores, and Amazon continued its machine march through consumable categories. All of it was fuel for the many "Sell!" recommendations.

Worse was how The Vitamin Shoppe was more than just another "tired retailer runs out of gas" story. There were historic regulatory concerns swirling around the category, as a few health supplement brands had been making dubious claims, and government regulators had gone after them hard. It didn't help that The Vitamin Shoppe, like its rival GNC, actually owned manufacturing assets and therefore was occasionally dragged into the crosshairs. As a result of these issues, the entire category and its two main publicly traded retailers were caught in a kind of "who's worse" ping-pong commentary by analysts and the media. Fair to say that all of it created a highly toxic environment in which to reinvent a business.

Thank goodness for data. It always reveals the truth of what *is*, and provides clues for what *might be*. In the case of the East Rutherford test store, data revealed a lot about the *might be* part, and it was incredibly compelling. As Watts shared, on every measure leadership could possibly care about—customer engagement and satisfaction, time spent in store, visit frequency, basket size (the term used in retail for the average spend per customer visit), penetration of new offerings alongside the core business of vitamins and supplements—everything went up. As a result, the freshly renovated store opened with a strong, double-digit lift in overall performance from its prior incarnation and was sustaining itself in the weeks that followed. In a category where specialty store performance was flat or in the low single-digit comp range, it was looking like a 10× improvement. And while the capital and operating expense of standing up any first prototype store are always on the high side—before value engineering and the economies that come from scale and refinement—the performance lift would likely deliver the required ROI when capital and expenses were normalized in "rollout," the term used in retail for scaling any initiative. Leadership now had a potential answer to the problem that had vexed the business for a decade: what to do with all those aging and underperforming stores in an age when customers could find whatever they needed online and for less. With some fine-tuning of the merchandising sets ("working the assortment and reworking the planograms," as the interim Chief Merchant, David Mock, would later say), there was broad confidence that East

Rutherford was the first large step in getting the business back to growth and a sustainably unique place in the world.

We suspected that what was driving these impressive results were two simple yet powerful insights:

1   Customers didn't need more products—those they could get anywhere. What they valued, and couldn't really find anywhere else, was help. Help with making decisions in a very complex category. Help with setting their goals, the primary driver of everything they did and purchased. Help to thrive, not as some final destination but as a daily journey.

2   Next, every product-related decision was viewed through this lens. The more it was solely about products, the more their decision making was naturally product-based, and that wasn't advantageous for The Vitamin Shoppe. Conversely, the more products came together with advice, support, and a community of peers learning and journeying together, the more it added up to real solutions. It was *solutions* customers were seeking.

Here was early proof that these insights were indeed unlocking a level of performance not seen in the business since its heyday and, even better, a level of customer engagement never before seen in the industry.

The reimagined store was a bright and welcoming place—the full facade had been opened up with windows, and the ceiling had been raised to accommodate better and brighter lighting. Categories of merchandise were organized by how customers wished to shop: by solutions, not by category. A "solutions table" was at the center of the store, a gathering place for one-on-one conversations and a forum for expert seminars, what we named "Spark Sessions." The store took the permission granted by customers to expand into fresh new categories, mostly high-frequency and growing offerings such as grab-and-go energy bars, functional beverages, prepared frozen meals, pre-packed ingredients for protein shakes, plus a curated selection of all-natural personal care and beauty products. The store included the world's first "kombucha growler bar," with happy hour events for socializing with like-minded goal-setters, and a protein powder sampling and refill center. As a result, the FROM/TO transformation was nothing short of jaw dropping. Customers' remarks from multiple store visits still ring in my ears, "This is a one-stop shop for my daily routines. Amazing!" "I can't believe how much I just learned." "This place is exactly what I was hoping for but sorry, I just didn't expect it from The Vitamin Shoppe." "I came in to grab some CoQ10 and spent a half hour discovering a whole world of options I didn't know existed."

For someone who helps brands get back to growth and relevance for a living, this was as good as it gets. Yet what was particularly cool and special about The Vitamin Shoppe, so very unusual in retail, was its store associates. Not only were the field team of "health enthusiasts" personally engaged with health and wellness, many of them were experts themselves. With degrees or designations in disciplines such as nutrition, naturopathy, and personal training, this was a group of people already equipped to add value, and most of them had been with the company a long time, much higher than the retail industry average. Here was the rare situation where the often-talked-about ideal of store associates providing expert advice to customers, helping beyond being friendly, and building genuine relationships with them, wasn't an unattainable dream but a real possibility. Truly this was a huge advantage, and the East Rutherford store was celebrating and amplifying it to great effect.

In that moment on stage in New York City as well as west through the Lincoln Tunnel to East Rutherford—all of this was true. The new store *was* a shining beacon of light in contrast to the dark horizon. Around that same time GNC was caught up in a firestorm, a shareholder uprising surrounding its debt load, further eroding category confidence and sending stock prices even lower. Amazon was stepping up its promotion and focus on vitamins and supplements, putting more pressure on profit, and making it crystal clear that digital was the new battlefield. And here was The Vitamin Shoppe, facing in real time the huge dilemma so many retailers struggle with today: reinvest in stores, the aging assets that are dragging down performance and ultimately must be addressed, or, invest in growth on digital platforms to take full advantage of the consumer channel shift to online? Tough choices made much tougher when the cupboards are bare. Yet now there was hope.

To be clear, I knew going in, as no doubt did Watts and others, that this one would not be easy. On the plus side, though, odds were moving in our collective favor on the basis of what had already been figured out:

- The business now had a deep understanding of customers and now knew what to *do* to be more, mean more, and therefore sell more to them

- There was clear white space for the brand to play within and win

- New offerings were resonating and punching above their weight

- Most encouraging, sales of core products sold since The Vitamin Shoppe's founding in 1977 were strong

- The local team in East Rutherford was reenergized, their enthusiasm off the charts

- Rich insights were emerging into how the store model could be further strengthened, as were ideas on where and how to take cost out

- In that single store—a proxy for what could be true across America in the future—credit for newness and innovation was accruing to the brand as never before

- The numbers showed it was working, and everyone was aligned on how to move forward

All of these points gave leadership the direction and confidence needed to press ahead. As Watts left the stage that day, I was thinking to myself from the audience: *nothing but up from here.*

But that didn't happen. As dark as the horizon was, and as strong as the headwinds against the business were, we had a strategy and it was working. In fact, it was really working. So why didn't that strategy, and the reinvention road map we had collaboratively laid out, take us back to growth? Why didn't it deliver The Vitamin Shoppe reborn?

The truth is it could have, but for one problem: we, everyone involved, got in our own way. While it took a while, and wasn't always apparent, it was human nature that stopped the reinvention of The Vitamin Shoppe. The uncertainty of it all was so strong and so pervasive that in the end it overcame every intention and every proof point and every bit of confidence.

There is much written about the "status quo bias," basically the idea that when left to our natural human inclinations, inertia will always win. What I think about most in the case of The Vitamin Shoppe was how collectively a decision was made to move forward with a bold plan, and at that moment there was a universally held belief that we knew where to go and were committed to get there. Yet over time, slyly yet steadily, the very human desire for *certainty* crept in.

Great start. But it could be a blip, so we will need more proof.

Okay, we have some strong results for reinventing stores, but our problem is coming from digital. Shouldn't we be making all our investments there?

Yes, there are some good things happening here. But there are a bunch of things that aren't working, and that's concerning.

Wow, this costs a lot of money. There's no way it can be scalable.

This is a big bet, and we need to be certain before we place it.

Let's slow down a bit and get this right.

Let's see how the competitive dynamics play out before we make another move.

Sound familiar? This is what status quo bias sounds like. With the benefit of hindsight, I can now see that *certainty* was a luxury the business could not afford. If the status quo, or some incrementally improved version of it, were a happy and productive spot for the foreseeable future, well then, we would have had permission to treat everything as discretionary. There would have been plenty of time to get it right before moving ahead. But it wasn't. The status quo wasn't an option in the least. Better to boldly take what was working and hone it, discard what wasn't working and replace it with what would, and keep going as fast as humanly possible.

Intentionally or not, we humans have a tendency to stop change. We nitpick and pull threads until the fabric comes apart. We sow seeds of doubt until people and plans wither. We tear down rather than build up. Or, we set the bar for success so high there is no chance it can be achieved. A common version of this is what I call *the expectation trap*, where we continue to forecast that performance will at least hold as it has. When it doesn't play out that way, the gap between what was promised and what can be delivered crushes confidence.

What we don't do is equally telling. Rather than asking, "Why are we protecting the status quo when it's not working?" we talk ourselves into going slow or returning to the safety of old ways. Even when the evidence clearly tells us we *have to move*—when our very survival depends upon it—our factory settings are hardwired to stay put. While we may shout "Go!" loud and decisively, we let all the doubts, all the small decisions, all the second-guessing and invisible resistance quietly add up to something else: *let's not*.

Looking back at The Vitamin Shoppe, we had it. We knew exactly where to go and had the road map to get there. And yet, once underway, we effectively pulled off to the side of the road and idled there until it was too late.

I must admit this story was hardest for me to write, as it's one of a few that got away. But I own the outcome as much as anyone, and fortunately there are lessons to take from it. What has stayed with me in the ensuing years is how there was, in one magical moment, unanimity amongst all of us on the way forward. Yet that alignment—as enthusiastic and evidence-based as it was—could not withstand the thousand cuts that would be inflicted on it along the way. Rather than courageously hitting the gas pedal, and keeping it there, honing our course as we went, we allowed caution to creep in, progress to slow until it stopped, and all confidence to wane. Uncertainty won. Now, you could say it was for a lot of good reasons. Except the one that mattered most: *time was up.*

For this reason alone, the only choice was to Embrace Uncertainty. To balance getting it right with getting on with it. For me, that's the lesson of the story.

AUTHOR's NOTE: *Within eighteen months of the opening of the East Rutherford store, the CEO, much of the Board and senior leadership team, and me and my team, were all gone from The Vitamin Shoppe, the result of an activist hedge fund catalyzing "urgent change." The business has now been taken private, and a new leadership team is working to develop their version of renewal. I wish them well, and my hope is that whichever course they choose they will courageously persevere.*

10

A stitch in time

The Joann story

WADE MIQUELON, formerly the CFO of Walgreens, rang me to say he had taken a new gig. He and I, along with former Walgreen's CEO Greg Wasson and his team, had a good run together collaborating on the reinvention of Walgreens, and I admired him as a big thinker. As the newly appointed CFO of Joann Stores, America's leading fabric and craft retailer, Miquelon and CEO Jill Soltau (now the CEO of JCPenney) were developing an overarching strategy for the business and the timing was right to talk about a store of the future. Although I was only generally aware of Joann, I was excited by the possibility of working with Miquelon again in a category that appeared to need some fresh thinking. My team and I had been on a multi-year tear reinventing drugstore and supermarket chains and we loved to cross-pollinate insights and inspiration from one category into another. I also appreciated that the business was owned by Leonard Green & Partners, a private equity firm I long admired but with whom I had yet to work.

While digital had become hugely important in the fabric and crafts category (as it is today in every corner of retail) and would be a key dimension of any reimagined experience for Joann customers, at the time the business was mainly store-based and the stores weren't performing. Joann had become another poster example of the crisis facing legacy retail, in particular big-box category killers and mall-based specialists—namely what to do with stores when customers no longer need or care to visit them. It wasn't as simple as replacing them with the digital alternative, considering that the hard truth of online/direct delivery is that few are making any money at it. This is the great paradox of retail today: online/direct is what more and more customers want and are migrating to, yet the all-in cost of actually doing it makes it a very challenging business model. For retailers to be profitable, at least for the foreseeable future, the go forward answer is omnichannel, including stores, as this is how and where money is made. Leaders like Miquelon and Soltau, the inheritors of almost 900 big-box stores across America, were left with only two options: figure out some new and magical way to compel customers to visit them more frequently, and spend more money each time, or eventually shutter a good many and hamper the ability to generate profit. Door A, an uncertain future. Door B... you don't want to go through Door B.

Coincidentally, the last "store of the future" I could recall visiting was a Walgreens I had toured in 2010 or so with some of Miquelon's former colleagues. At the time, I was onboarding to assist with the transformation of that business after the acquisition of Duane Reade. If you had traveled with me and popped into Walgreens stores from coast to coast, across middle America to its hometown of Chicago, you would have discovered, as I did, pretty much the same store wherever you went. Walgreens wasn't a collection of 8,000+ stores as much as one store replicated 8,000 times. Yet here, in a northeast suburb of Chicago, was an unusual store where the layout was different, the décor was different, and many of the offerings were unique. Yet, like some kind of experimental aircraft flown once and then mothballed, no other store like it was ever built. When I asked why this was the case, I heard a familiar refrain:

There were mixed results. It wasn't a home run.

Too expensive, so not replicable.

Not everyone agreed on what we were trying to accomplish.

Too much change, so hard to imagine how we could get it to scale.

In big business (or in the case of Walgreens, a BIG business) reliability and predictability are valued above all, and a store of the future—exciting but often experimental and lacking any strategic underpinning—had uncertainty written all over it. Throwing stuff at the wall to see what sticks seldom leads to any kind of certainty or sustainable breakthrough.

At Joann at least there was certainty and alignment on one point: leadership needed a fix to their store challenge. Everything beyond that was naturally uncertain. How much change was necessary? How much would it cost? Would the investment be worth it? Would people come along with it? What would happen if it didn't work? If it did, would the economics be right to scale it? These were all reasonable questions, and any one of them alone was capable of bringing a lofty initiative to the ground in a hurry. Uncertainty is, after all, a killer.

So rather than calling it "store of the future" we opted for a term I picked up from Glenn Murphy, back when he was Chairman and CEO of Gap Inc. Miquelon and Soltau agreed we would pursue a "brand-defining store." Rather than frame it as a free-standing initiative and strategy, we would make it a complete manifestation of *one cohesive strategy*. In doing so we avoided the silo trap, where good solutions are arrived at independently but never ladder up to brand. We also agreed that what we set out to do we would *do boldly*, and it would either work, or we would learn from it and refine it until it did. We would do it collaboratively. We would work with real data and human insights. We would rapidly test early hypotheses. And we would make the big strategic choices together *before* we put pen to paper.

Looking back, the approach we took immunized us against the insidious threat of uncertainty. In the end, innovation is a battle in the mind between *can* and *cannot*. This is what *can* looked like at Joann:

We went digging for insights and found one we could hang an entire strategy on, namely that *humans are all hardwired to create and SHARE*. It takes effort to uncover insights, and it takes courage to fully get behind one once you discover it.

We studied the facts for what they could reveal, yet equally trusted our feelings, embracing the idea that the future is not an extrapolation of the past but an intervening creative act.

We tested hypotheses in a matter of weeks, in the scrappiest ways possible. The lessons learned and the additional data we collected helped us to hone our strategy and prove our thesis. On the strength of this clarity and our collective conviction, the Board blessed a bold new strategy to accelerate Joann toward a winning position and endorsed the building of a brand-defining store—the "BDS" as it would come to be known—in Columbus, Ohio.

We did a brave thing and took almost 20 percent of the square footage of that store, space formerly devoted to merchandise density, and gave it back to customers in community space and a learning environment called The Creators' Studio. We were paid back many times over.

We challenged the convention of the industry and category, reinventing everything from the way fabric bolts were displayed (upsetting a century-old tradition) to the role of associates, from shelf stockers to the *friendly clever allies* that would help customers conceive of and do anything.

We spent multiple times the capital of a typical store renovation to build the Columbus store, and the main decision makers, Soltau and Miquelon, did it without blinking.

We never bowed to the daunting scope of what we set out to do. We just broke it down into chunks and steps, stayed true to strategy, locked our eyes on the prize, and kept up the pace. Importantly, we brought an ever-widening circle of people along with us and made it theirs as much as ours.

We measured every bit of what we did. When results came back showing a massive double-digit improvement in comp store sales performance (along with a bigger average basket size, increased shopping frequency, greater customer satisfaction, and a meaningful bump in revenue from new services like The Custom Shop), we celebrated and doubled down.

What to take from this story? Uncertainty causes doubt. It fuels fear. It slows progress and stops reinvention. Do not let it. By embracing uncertainty, the new leadership at Joann opened up to possibilities that changed the entire business. They fearlessly tried new ways and were not embarrassed in the least when some of them did not work out as planned. They simply went back and refined them until they did, or gracefully let them go and got onto the next thing. And, they did it all before time ran out.

11

Third Mindset Principle

Create the Future Now

THE FUTURE. It just sounds like a far-off place. When I was a kid, the word "future" conjured up BIG things. A fantastical world of flying cars and space travel, say. Or a life of adventures and possibilities far beyond what I knew. Whatever my future would turn out to be I was sure it would be quite different, and I think this is how many of us grew up and thought about it. The future was a liftoff of some kind, a dramatic change in trajectory—*to infinity and beyond!*—rather than a more natural path from past to present to what's next. It is only when I look back on things that I realize the so-called big leaps in my career were perhaps more logical than I initially thought. When viewed from 50,000 feet and in hindsight, there has been a purposeful progression from who and what I was, to what I dreamt I could be, to what I became. It's an important distinction I think; the future is what happens when you move through that simple sequence, and it keeps unfolding when you continue.

The opposite way is to resist. To see and treat pretty much every move forward as a significant departure from the norm and therefore a BIG decision, weighted with risk and gravitas. It isn't "What if it doesn't work?" that slows things down, but rather "What if it does?" Played out, this causes the future to be viewed as not only scary but optional. "Sorry, everyone. We've rescheduled the future. It won't be happening until the timing suits us. We will reschedule it when conditions are right and we can be certain it won't be so disruptive."

There are many ways to consciously or subconsciously try to prevent the future from coming, and all of them are laughable. I'm reminded of the Grinch, who determined he "must stop Christmas from coming!" The future arrives regardless of our attitude and readiness for it. What we miss during all this avoidance, done in the name of prudence, is that when the future does arrive, as it always does, our readiness for it depends in great part on whether or not we had a hand in shaping it.

Imagine two hypothetical companies with a similar business model, and each about to be impacted by technology. One begins experimenting with new ways to apply technology to its business in small ways, learning from its failures while growing comfortable with the tools and possibilities. The other resists and procrastinates, seeing in the technology only unreasonable expense and a threat to its very way of doing things. Which do you think had the better chance of evolving into the future when the world shifted, technology became cheaper and more pervasive, and technology-led start-ups began arriving on the scene?

We all have a choice. But unless we actively do the choosing, decisions get made for us. This too is human nature. Unless we happen to be hardwired entrepreneurs, the majority of us build things not to tear them down and rebuild them, but to see them maintained. We protect what we have built because, well, *we built it*. And from whom are we protecting it? From those who would do it differently. From those who think there is a better version. From those unreasonable people upon whom all progress relies. In short, we're protecting it from the future. As crazy as this may sound, it's true. Today in the business zeitgeist there is this idea floating around that everyone needs to "future-proof" their business. Yikes. We don't need to future-proof our businesses, to prevent bad and unknown things from happening to them. We need to actively engage in writing our own futures, to be *authors of the unknown* and therefore in control of our own stories. The only thing we should want to protect is the story itself, no matter where it leads. The only thing we should fear is getting stuck in any particular chapter, bringing the book to a precipitous end. Alan Kay, formerly Chief Scientist at Atari and member of the famed Xerox PARC organization, famously said, "The best way to predict the future is to invent it." I would add: the best way to ensure it's to your liking is to continually reinvent it and do it quickly.

Here is how to *Create the Future Now*:

- **Pay attention.** It's a straight build from Seek Insight Everywhere. Tune in to what is happening around you at present. What are your customers asking for and complaining about? How are your associates responding and what do they see as opportunity? If there are things that appear to matter, they likely do.

- **Never wait.** If you see change coming your way, or an opportunity to create change yourself, do it. And do it fast. The world isn't waiting for you to get your act together. Put things in motion. Simulate the future now. A sidebar to your business can turn out to *be* your business, but only if you are the one who gives it a try. You'll never have to bet the farm if you keep planting and harvesting future seeds.

- **Distinguish between doing things to win and doing things to learn.** Stop making everything about performance improvement and financial metrics. This forces you into a predictable mode of making only functional refinements. While this is an essential discipline, it must be paired with a more expansive view of what's possible. Continually exploring creative new ways to engage and satisfy customers—trying things beyond the obvious, beyond your current model—are where the game changers of the future live.

- **Have fun.** The future is exciting, and it is both a privilege and a blast to be a part of figuring it out. Be sure to fully participate with the right attitude, and help others do the same.

12

The new mix of fun

The Dave & Buster's story

A FEW YEARS AFTER the sale of Duane Reade to Walgreens, I received a call from Tyler Wolfram of Oak Hill Capital Partners. "Jackman. Meet me in New Jersey. There's someone I want you to meet." This would turn out to be the second time I visited the New York City area and couldn't wait to jump back on a plane home. (The first time, of course, being my initial look at the old Duane Reade.)

Steve King was a good guy, if at first a little guarded and naturally wary of a consultant being introduced to him by a Board member and owner. He walked me around a typical Dave & Buster's, a dark wood and brassy museum of arcade games past, with the faint odor of worn broadloom and stale popcorn and the discomforting sadness found only in empty casinos at midday. Nearly alone in the dining room, the three of us sat down for a chat over burgers, wings, poppers, fries, and iced tea. (There was a reasonable chance that this engagement, if it came to pass, would kill me.)

Twenty years before, Dave & Buster's was a red-hot rocket ship. It couldn't build locations fast enough across America: Boston, Philadelphia, Chicago, Oakland, Honolulu. The unlikely start of the business came in Little Rock, Arkansas, when the owners of two separate joints noticed their respective clientele moving back and forth to play arcade games and grab a bite. Bingo. Dave Corriveau and James "Buster" Corley teamed up and opened their first combo establishment in Dallas, Texas, in 1982.

Dave & Buster's was truly in a category of one. No other venue at the time combined an eye- and ear-popping arcade with cheap and cheerful food and a TGI Fridays–like bar. Skeeball, shoot a hoop, pinball, shooting galleries, and games of chance... all offering a chance to win buckets of tickets redeemable for "fabulous" prizes. Grab a drink. Play some games. Hit the dinner tables for some yummy food and maybe a wink across the bar. It was a hit with young people looking to cut loose and play for bragging rights, parents passing time with their kids, and the office gang kicking back for some after-hours fun. Dave and Buster had designed "the country club for the rest of us," and it printed money for well over two decades.

Yet the Dave & Buster's that King now led was a shadow of its former self. Minus 6 percent year over year sales declines when he took the reins. Dwindling traffic, even amongst the die-hard brand lovers. Worse—in a sea of casual restaurant/bar options promoting cheap eat/drink combos, and a technology revolution that put the latest and greatest games at people's fingertips—Dave & Buster's was a relic, relegated to office parties and the occasional hit of nostalgia.

After a good stretch of his career spent in finance at Darden Restaurants, King joined Dave & Buster's as CFO at a time of steady free fall. He and his team began taking cost out and looking for efficiencies, and soon after, as the newly appointed CEO, he doubled down on operational improvements and began bringing in talent from outside, something the company hadn't done in quite some time. The efforts over two years of hard work yielded a whopping seven-point swing in sales. Yet +1 percent—a little better than flat sales—didn't make for a very compelling story. No matter how valiant his efforts, the business was treading water when a return to robust growth was the plan. At that moment, amongst the long, late afternoon shadows in a tired venue in New Jersey, Wolfram and King were looking for answers.

As the lunch came to a close, King asked a question: "After everything we've done it's not enough. What's possible from here?"

As I made my way back to the airport, I couldn't see the way forward on this one. With regard to pretty much every major consumer trend, Dave & Buster's was offside. The heavily built-out, aging assets would require a lot of capital for even a small dent in customer experience. (Most private equity partners don't like that, the general rule being that capital is for buying companies, not reinventing them.) The food was mediocre and undifferentiated, the staff were great people but seemed stuck in a time warp, and the latest games that consumers were obsessed with were nowhere in sight (it took thirty days for 50 million people to download the Angry Birds app, yet at that time the game was unlikely to be in a Dave & Buster's for at least a year). This point was the most troubling: What to do with yesterday's idea of fun? I practically ran back to the plane.

All the way home I was phrasing and rephrasing how I would tell Wolfram that I wouldn't take the gig. No doubt it would be a challenging conversation. In my world, good relations with the captains of industry who buy and sell businesses are important, and Wolfram and I had established a good rapport after the lucrative sale of Duane Reade to Walgreens. But successful reinvention is not a certainty. In every deal, I take a sizable financial stake (by my standards) and this bet would be long odds.

I was persuaded to take the gig.

Fast-forward three years and Dave & Buster's was winning again. With a focus on the PTYAs, short for "Play Together Young Adults," defined by age but more importantly by mindset and attitude toward socializing, we had hit the sweet spot. Freshly renovated locations were jammed until the wee hours, not only with young people but older cohorts that shared the same values. The associates had upped their game and were totally into it. The food and drinks were better. The environment was cooler and celebrated the brand and its unique origin story. Everyone was rocking the latest and greatest games, some of which were completely exclusive to Dave & Buster's. Sports fans were cheering on their favorite teams in the newly created D&B Sports zone, with giant screens and leaderboards. All in all, the buzz was back. From a business perspective, the real estate pipeline of new locations, a vital factor in future growth, was once again full of promising prospects, and an impressive two-year comparable sales lift of +20 percent drove a successful IPO.

Wait. How the heck did that happen? Well, King is a very capable CEO, and Wolfram is a visionary guy. Most vitally though, and to the point: almost thirty years after its founding, we all rediscovered what made Dave & Buster's great in the first place, its DNA—a unique mix of immersive fun and food, the latest and greatest games, and the pure joy of playing together. We used it, along with insights on socialization and fun that we uncovered, to creatively reimagine the value proposition and end-to-end customer experience. We were bold. We did it fast. We didn't let the past hold us back. In fact, we used it to pivot us forward. We didn't wait for the future to arrive, we simply got busy creating it.

Stasis

Over three decades and counting I continue to be surprised by how little most businesses actually evolve year over year, even when the world around them is changing weekly. Even when evidence is piling up that the "same old, same old" no longer cuts it.

There isn't a single reason for this natural stasis, but three.

First, we hang on to what we know for too long, succumbing to that strong human need for reliability and predictability. Certainty is comfort, and comfort preserves the status quo.

Second, generally speaking, we humans have an aversion to effort. If given a choice, we'll take the path of least resistance. It's just easier to leave things as they are rather than get busy with the heavy lifting.

Third, there are the financial rewards that come with making little or no change, at least for a time. A business that hasn't done much innovating in a while, with the accompanying investment that goes with it, is harvesting what has previously been sown. This might be considered smart in the early going, and it's tempting to keep going with what could reasonably be termed "overperformance" for as long as possible. But even while everyone looks like a genius for a while it is a falsehood. Past a certain point, starving a business of reinvestment to sustain high returns, which happens all the time, shouldn't be called genius but milking it dry. It never ends well.

You can choose stasis for any number of reasons. Just know that a steep tab is on its way to your table when you do.

13

Reinventing a reinvention company

The Jackman Reinvents story

WHEN I LEFT Loblaw Companies, after a few years "client side," I had a decision to make: stay in the corporate world, or return to consulting. I chose the latter because I knew I could add more value on the outside than from within, and I was now on a mission.

In 2007, I started a consulting firm specializing in reinvention. Nothing like it existed at the time. The idea came to me before I left Loblaw, in a meeting with several McKinsey consultants, a few creative folks, and members of my own marketing team. We had gathered to discuss and hopefully solve a problem facing the business, and it was clear that none of us used the same frameworks, spoke the same language, or shared any commonality on how to approach and resolve a challenge. The consequence was misalignment and lost time, time we didn't have. It was at that moment that I had an epiphany, another AHA moment: The worlds of business strategy, brand strategy, and customer understanding and experience should be united. There should and could be a way to seamlessly bring these disciplines together AND do it in such a way as to enable change to happen more efficiently and cohesively.

When I started Jackman, the firm, I could picture it. I brought together all the disciplines needed for reinvention under one roof—researchers, management consultants, brand strategists, marketers, designers, writers, and activation managers—and got us all focused on *making change possible*. And a wonderful thing happened. We were given the opportunity to do some once-in-a-lifetime transformational work by a few visionary leaders that understood what we were trying to do and were willing to take a chance on us. It grew. So much so that demand began to outstrip supply. Within only a few short years we were 100+ Reinventionists and we were winning.

Then, something inexplicable happened. Something I did not see coming.

My business stopped working the way it had done for close to a decade. All the things I cared about as a leader were off: top-line sales, profit margin, quality of work going out the door, the pipeline of new opportunities, and, most importantly, employee satisfaction. I could hear myself complaining about my own business in the same way leaders of companies I was helping to reinvent did about theirs: "On every dimension that counts, the business is severely underperforming." Yikes. Here I was, now an expert at getting companies back to growth and relevance, and yet my own business was faltering. If there was ever a professional out-of-body experience, this was it.

I share this story with you for a reason: change comes calling whether we like it or not. It is never convenient, and no one is immune. The trouble is we all have been conditioned to not deviate when things are working, until at some point they stop working. We presume we have it right for all time and that a tweak here or there will keep us on a successful track. Even when we see warning signs, as I did, we ignore them. This is a pattern that repeats itself across every company and every industry.

Now, having experienced it firsthand, I can say I didn't like it one bit. I didn't like that it took me by surprise; I just presumed things would return to how they had been. I didn't like that it forced me to revisit pretty much everything in my business: my strategy; the operating model; leadership and the organizational model; the standards of work; and the value proposition itself. I didn't like the financial hit I was taking, as revenue flattened and cost as a percentage of sales therefore grew. I didn't like the price tag that would come with restructuring. And, I sure didn't like the optics. My reputation was and is important to me. Least of all, I didn't like the hard decisions I had to make about people. Ultimately, I let a number of good ones go and a few of them were friends.

Does any or all of this sound familiar? It's painful. But nevertheless, I took my medicine and only wished I had done it sooner. Together with my Advisory Board Chairman David Moore, and my colleagues David Zietsma and Sandra Duff, we simplified the leadership and operating structure of my business. We took cost out where it didn't count and reinvested where it did. We pushed authority down so that those who DO were empowered and fully owned the work. We retooled compensation so we were all in for the win together. We simplified the playbook of how to reinvent from start to finish. We refined our strategy. We expanded activation capabilities so we could move faster and up the odds of successful outcomes. And, we did it all by honoring our own principles, by living the Reinventionist Mindset, and by applying our unique method to ourselves.

Reflecting on the experience—of reinventing a reinvention company— I realize that all the things I didn't like about making change were additional reasons why the status quo lived longer than it should have. Expense. Optics. Difficulty. Energy. Uncertainty. I pushed change out further and further for what I thought were good reasons, until it bit me in the backside.

Yet, mine was and is a small business. As challenging as all that was, how much more difficult would it have been if it was a large, publicly traded enterprise with a lot more eyeballs on it? Or if my business were owned by private equity, with annual growth and EBITDA (net profit) targets set against an investment thesis? I say this not to diminish what I faced and ultimately dealt with, but to illustrate that varying circumstances bring varying degrees of difficulty. I can only imagine if my decisions affected thousands of people and their livelihoods. Change is hard for everyone. Not making change is ultimately harder though, and the implications are graver. What I've come to understand is why leaders hang on for so long. We hope things will naturally work themselves out. We make excuses to delay the inevitable for as long as possible, as I certainly did. But when we delay, things don't get better. They get worse. Change gets harder and more expensive.

There are two lessons to this story. The first is never wait. Accept that change is the normal and natural order of things and get on with it. Secondly, change before you are forced to. Create the Future Now and keep doing it.

AUTHOR'S NOTE: *In case you were worried about how this particular story ended, my business was almost completely retooled and was returned to growth and even greater traction. Sometimes the shoemaker does have nice shoes.*

When do you know it is time for reinvention?

While it's clear that change is coming more quickly than before, knowing this doesn't answer the question that faces every business leader: When is the time to make change yourself? The best overall diagnostic is to understand where your business is within its life cycle—still in *growth phase*, nearing *maturity*, at its *peak*, or already in *decline*?—and to use that to determine the timing of reinvention:

- **Growth phase**: Calls for continual honing and refinement.
- **Maturity**: This is "Position A" for beginning reinvention.
- **Peak**: This is "Position B," the fallback start if you haven't already begun to reinvent.
- **Decline**: You've left things for too long, so now it's time for "hurry up" offense and reinvention on steroids.

Businesses should begin their reinvention toward the end of the growth phase or at the beginning of the maturity phase, effectively figuring out their next act before the current one comes to a close. If you've gone past both of these points in your life cycle, or past the peak, you need to move fast.

Here are the telltale signs beyond general performance erosion that reinvention is necessary or overdue:

Growth from the core business has disappeared or is slowing. If every initiative to maintain growth means adding a new offering or jumping into an adjacent category, the core may be broken, has lost its relevance, or both. For example, growth in Gap brand's core jeans business had slowed in the 2000s, and it drove the company to pursue other categories such as workwear and athletic apparel with marginal success.

A variation of this is dependence upon geographic expansion to continue to grow the business. Successful businesses are those that are growing within their footprint as well as expanding it.

The business or brand isn't being talked about anymore. When your business has become like a great aunt, kindly thought of yet taken for granted and seldom visited. Great brands and businesses insinuate their way into the imagination, manufacture news, and habitually draw attention to themselves. The chatter needn't be universally affectionate— better to be controversial than ignored! An example here would be Walgreens before its reinvention: the ubiquitous chain store on every corner was like wallpaper.

The business adheres faithfully to the rules of the category. Sorry, there is no way to sugarcoat this one. Having no meaningful differentiation between a business and its competitors isn't a sustainable position.

I have seen this in almost every category, from drugstores and super-markets to restaurants. Before its reinvention Hertz was a good example, where data revealed very little perceptual and actual difference between Hertz and its main rivals, unless you counted yellow as different from red, orange, and green.

The category itself is without growth, or in decline. Sometimes entire categories are made irrelevant by the changing competitive landscape, and every business within the category suffers. Take the casual dining restaurant category, where year-over-year growth has slowed to a trickle due in part to the emergence of the "fast casual" category of restaurants like Chipotle. In this instance, the brand and category are being disrupted by a new model. There is a new and exciting kid in town making everyone look bad. It's not anything the business has done—it's what is being done to the business.

The most valuable customers are older. Unless your business is specif-ically targeting older audiences, such as a seniors' home, it's likely risking irrelevance with every year that passes. If younger people are not attracted to a business, it simply has no future, and even those serving older consumers must be aware that they are swimming upstream. I've faced this challenge with leaders in almost every category. The average age of Canadian Tire's core customers was steadily creeping up without sufficient replacement by younger cohorts until the leadership team went after it with fulsome customer experience improvement.

For those businesses *past* the growth phase, reinvention is overdue. The obvious point here is to never wait that long. It is infinitely more diffi-cult, and always much more expensive, to reboot a mature business or reverse one already in a tailspin.

The greatest irony in all of this is that the time to reinvent roughly coincides with or precedes the moment when things are going swimmingly. In other words, the time to suit up for battle again is just before the victory party begins.

———

14

Fourth Mindset Principle

Obsess the Outcome

J OSHUA TREE National Park, one of the most spiritual places in America, was named by the earliest Mormon pioneers on their way west. The outstretched arms of the trees native to the desert there brought to mind the biblical Joshua beckoning travelers to the promised land. In the face of the most inhospitable of conditions, this reminder of their destination reassured and compelled them forward on their journey. Such is the value of a clear and present outcome, particularly when the going is tough.

In his novel *War and Peace*, Tolstoy penned, "One needs a vision of the promised land in order to have the strength to move." The implicit idea being that movement from one place to a better one is almost always filled with trials and tribulations. Therefore, picturing it—the land of milk and honey, with its comforts and rewards—is essential to conjuring the will to overcome the barriers standing in the way of achieving it. It's a pretty simple yet powerful idea, and it plays out in ancient stories as well as modern times. "Mom, are we there yet?" "Not yet, but just think about how wonderful it's going to be when we get to the beach!" Grand or trivial, we humans are willing to put up with a lot when we can picture in our minds the happy place we are headed toward. "Seeing it" has the psychological effect of making it real and therefore hastens our movement toward it.

This concept of picturing and then obsessively focusing on achieving an intended outcome is one of the keys to reinvention. Every substantial business transformation brings with it a great many challenges, and the first and most formidable of these is convincing a community of people that it is time to change. Individuals, no matter where they sit within an organization, each have their own views on what is and is not worthwhile, their own tolerance for discomfort, and their own bias toward or against change. Organizations are human ecosystems, and as such each participant is in a position to directly impact, or at least influence, the entire outcome by offering his or her full support, actively working against it, or something in between.

Think about it. In reinvention we are fundamentally asking people to let go of current reality—*their reality,* with all its familiar and reassuring ways of doing things—to take a leap to bring about change. If your colleagues are not fully convinced the journey will be worth the risk, or if they are simply comfortable where they are and would rather stay there, your progress will be slower. You may be prevented from achieving your outcome altogether. Without the majority in support and moving forward with you, your chances of implementing a strategy—no matter how brilliant it may be—are just about zero. Worse, given that time is a luxury most businesses cannot afford, directional alignment and motivation cannot be left to chance.

In my experience, you can take any community of people and divide them into three groups. There's the 20 percent *movers,* those who are excited by change and enjoy a challenge. Then you've got the 20 percent *stoppers,* those who will fight hard to protect the status quo every step of the way, particularly if they see it as an affront to the past or a threat to their livelihood or status. And last, there's that big group in between, the *momentous middle,* the 60 percent whose minds will be made up based upon what they see, hear, and come to believe. In other words, they are the vital majority to swing your way in any reinvention. The general rule is this: you want the movers pushing forward *in your direction* (a predilection for change doesn't guarantee fidelity to a particular path, it just means they like to move), you want the stoppers neutralized or taken out entirely (as Jim Collins framed it so well, "off the bus"), and you want the momentous middle inspired, aligned, and in motion.

In transformations of any kind, this is "make or break" stuff: Strategies fail when the humans who populate your organization cannot easily grasp the need for the journey (the "why"), the place where it leads to (the "where"), some sense of the path to get there (the "how"), and the reward for all the hard traveling ahead (the "what"). If they're not clear on the answers, they have reason not to join you.

No matter how well conceived, strategy is worthless if it cannot be implemented. Therefore, the human factor is large and consequential. Yet most strategies, by their rational and narrowly defined nature, fail the most basic test of all. They are not built to excite people about an *outcome* and show them the way to reach it. Conventionally built business strategies tend to be all *how* with minimal *why*, but they also fall short on the *where* and *what*. Making change possible rests on all four dimensions.

Allow me to explain it this way:

Why. This is all about making a clear *case for change*, a simple yet essential explanation of why we need to move, whether skewed negative ("we are threatened and can no longer stay where we are") or positive ("there is a better, more worthwhile place for us to go"), or both. *Why* counts in reinvention because the more we humans understand the reasons for change the more we feel respected and are open to it. If you are from the old "command-and-control" school of thinking, believing you can simply order *your* people to execute *your* strategy, I can't offer you much, except to say you would be wise to revisit this approach.

Where. This is the outcome you are working toward. A depiction, ideally a story and visualization alongside financial coordinates, of the place you are going and will thrive. It is not enough to frame a business outcome in financial terms alone, as so many strategies and plans still do. Reinvention requires us to engage *head and heart* together. The consequence of narrowing the appeal to the head alone—facts and figures only—ignores the most powerful force of human nature: emotions. As we know well, the heart wants what the heart wants and its potential to overcome obstacles is formidable. So why wouldn't we fully engage and channel that force? When we do, we have the full power of human nature on our side.

How. This is the path and specific actions you will take to achieve your destination. Not just big steps, but small ones that confirm and demonstrate direction, and early ones that put you on your way and get everyone used to moving ahead. Stating intentions is easy. You need to get specific on *how and when*, and a road map that shows the way forward in a step-by-step sequence is vital.

What. As in, what *benefits* will result? Not just in financial terms but in more deeply resonant ways. Reinvention comes down to motivation. We need to sell not only the dream but the benefits of the dream, and the more meaningful the benefits are, the more magnetic the dream becomes. One has only to look at Maslow's Hierarchy of Needs (Abraham Maslow's theory of human motivation first published in *Psychological Review* in 1943) to understand that we humans seek meaning in our lives. When we believe there is a higher order benefit to be achieved, our inclination to join the journey goes up. In other words, tell them about the milk and honey again, and how we will all be happy in this place.

Reinvention isn't just a strategic and financial exercise, it's a human one. Therefore, we need to frame this powerful idea of "outcome" in human terms. The more people understand why they are moving toward an outcome, what it looks like, how it will be achieved, and the benefits of reaching it, the more they will be motivated to obsess over it.

15

The great American food dream

The US Foods story

N 2010, US Foodservice, as it was then known, was a substantial if unexciting business, with little differentiation or competitive advantage to speak of. At $20+ billion in annual sales, distributing food to restaurants, hotels, hospitals, and even the armed services, it was— for all its scale and national market position, and all the daily efforts of thousands of associates focused on taking care of customers— simply running fast to stay in place. When newly established leadership brought my team in to help transform the business, the reality was sobering. No strategy, no growth, no fun.

Perhaps what I am describing sounds familiar. There are a lot of businesses out there like US Foodservice once was. It was born in an era when standing up a decent business—meaning, decently competent and reasonably efficient—and scaling it in sync with a rising tide of market growth was all that was required to succeed. Pick any category and think of the players within it: airlines (American, Delta, United), car rental companies (Avis, Hertz, Enterprise), casual restaurants (Applebee's, Chili's, TGI Fridays) drugstores (CVS, Rite Aid, Walgreens), supermarkets (Kroger, Safeway, Albertsons), telcos (Sprint, T-Mobile, Verizon). What they all had in common was that they were giants, together controlled the lion's share of the market, and, if any upstarts came along, they simply absorbed or crushed them. Oh yeah. They were all exact replicas of one another. You could describe this reality as the natural order of things, at least up to the turn of the last century. And this was exactly the case with the foodservice category and the two players within it, US Foodservice and its larger rival Sysco.

The natural order I mention is somewhat shocking though, when viewed through a twenty-first-century lens. A gaggle of big and very similar businesses taking advantage of a naturally expanding landscape, noting that the American economy grew from $0.3 trillion in 1950 to $10.25 trillion in 2000. Occasionally one player or another might take some share this way or that, but basically the main players just divided the market and surfed the wave. I recall a Canadian bank executive explaining it to me this way: "There are five of us that divide up the market, and we are all roughly interchangeable with each other. Fortunately, customers don't like to switch banks often, which helps to preserve our natural market share." Natural market share? That is a comforting notion, but a completely outdated one in today's hypercompetitive and disruptive reality. It does, however, explain how so many businesses, like US Foodservice, got along for so long without really having a unique strategy. It was just the norm.

The end of the party for US Foodservice, and so many businesses like it, arrived circa 2000, when the barriers surrounding the big players in every category began crumbling and then came crashing down thanks to technology. Want to broadcast to millions of people without the hassle of building a media network or selling to one? No issue, here's a bunch of social media platforms to give you reach and amplification. Want to become a retailer, and sell directly to consumers without ever having to get into the messy business of being the middleman? Go for it, just sign up here with Shopify and Square, and incentivize the heck out of those influencers to get the word out. Want to create your own brand and take it to market, from design to global manufacturing to distribution? Welcome to the world of outsourcing and the gig economy. Want to start a hotel business without buying a piece of real estate? Build an app that connects owners with renters. Every one of these scenarios is technology-enabled of course, and every one of them is taking real share from the old guard that at one time owned it all. And it's just getting started.

This is where US Foodservice sat for a decade, the second-place victor of a food distribution land grab. With pricing pretty much the same across the market, and few if any ways to distinguish itself. The national and big regional players had similar fleets of trucks and distribution centers; the same ways of interacting with customers; and, roughly the same offerings (even in "center of plate," where offerings like meat and seafood are most strategically important). They all had underdeveloped brands, and customer loyalty rested upon whether an independent restaurateur, or purchasing agent at one of the big restaurant chains, was up for the hassle of switching suppliers if and when something went wrong. US Foodservice came up short about as often as its competitors did, so it and their "natural market share" prevailed. It goes without saying that being least-worst is not a sound strategy.

As I got into it with their leadership and my team, something interesting jumped out from the data. In the rankings of what was important to customers in the foodservice industry, innovation was dead last. We had never seen this in any other category. Typically, innovation, or "newness" of one kind or another, would be somewhere in the middle of the pack, below more universal expectations of price and convenience, yet above typically low-expectation attributes such as expert advice. But in this case, the data was clearly saying customers didn't value innovation whatsoever. How could that be? A deeper dive revealed that when it came to product innovation, the national and big regional players were slow to bring new food ideas to market. Why would anyone value something they could never expect? This was a big and potentially pivotal market insight.

In an era where interest in food was at an all-time high, with chefs as celebrities and entire media networks devoted to food, it typically took years for even big trends, like natural/organic or the latest flavors from around the world, to make their way to foodservice—if ever. What if, instead of being all about trucks and warehouses and deliveries, US Foodservice became all about food innovation? What if the business could bust out of the pack, do the unexpected, and actually innovate? Here was an AHA hiding in plain sight, and better still, it resonated with a vibrant DNA strand of the business, a love of food dating back to the earliest days when some of the most food-centric companies were brought together to form

US Foodservice in the 1980s. Versus its twice-the-size rival Sysco, could the business truly be *first in food and second to none*? By doing so, could it connect more powerfully with customers, who data revealed also shared a deep and abiding love of food, and wanted to be on trend with what was happening in the world? Now *that* was a worthwhile dream.

Dreams, however, are not reality. Unless, of course, they are *held up as the outcome you set your sights on, obsess over, and pursue relentlessly*. Unless you decide, as leadership did in this case, to simply start living that dream and become it.

So here's what we all did to make the dream a reality:

We focused on the customer segment that loves food most, the independent restaurateur—the one that sets the trends and every other segment looks to for new ideas.

We made everything about the love of food and aligned *everything* to it, resulting in a complete realignment of our plans and priorities.

We celebrated our love of food culturally and created a "Food Fanatics" designation for the best chefs in the business, which many of the sales force were previously in their careers, personifying and amplifying their passion and expertise. We began publishing a magazine under the same name and brought customer chefs into a community of food love and new ideas.

We stood up a product development team and world-class test kitchen from scratch, and launched a flagship "exclusive brand" called Chef's Line, bringing real innovation to the foodservice market and amplifying our commitment to food leadership.

We named meeting rooms after famous chefs and reinforced what we were about on every screen saver and every redesigned coffee mug.

We re-imaged the business, from the red, white, and blue of America to the summer green and citrus orange of beautiful food. We changed every truck and every uniform and every business card and every sign on every building and gave all of it a new name: US Foods. Where US Foodservice spoke to the industry, with an emphasis on trucks and warehouses, US Foods spoke to people about a shared love of food. It shouted that we were the great American food company that happened to be in the foodservice business.

The outcome we all focused on and obsessed over became real. US Foods got back to growth by developing a real strategy, unlike so many big and undifferentiated companies in so many other categories. It drew a line around a new category and became first in it, so much so that its main rival and market leader Sysco tried to acquire it (again proving that market leaders sit up and take notice when competitors do different things, and often try to buy them). Ultimately, the FTC deemed that the transaction was not to be, and in May of 2016, US Foods was successfully taken public in the second-largest offering of that year. The point of the story? Dreams do become reality if you obsess over them.

How to successfully communicate through reinvention

Let's face it. Most strategies are dry as toast, a collection of objectives and tactics and PowerPoint slides. Worse, by the very nature of their content, they can come off in a kind of "talk down" way that frankly turns people off. Updates on progress can also be deadly dull. It needn't be this way, and it shouldn't be if your intention is to capture the heads and hearts of everyone and, in doing so, get to success faster.

Here are a few things I've learned from communicating in transformational situations that can make a big difference:

Stories motivate us. Learn how to weave all your facts and figures and intentions into a simple and relatable story, a human one that will inspire people, and to which you can return again and again. Better to tell and sell the arc of a compelling story, and then go deeper with content in various chapters as appropriate. If you're not able to do it yourself, don't dismiss it, just get someone to help write it with you. Sharing your ambitions and plans in story form will resonate more deeply with everyone on your team. Who knows, you may even surprise yourself with how engaging you and your content can be.

Pictures motivate us. Don't just share it, show it. Make your intentions as tangible as possible. Adding more images to enhance and humanize content also engages people in deeper ways. Seeing is believing ... and believing will cause everyone to see it through to a successful outcome.

Endorsement motivates us. Don't share and show it alone, share and show it together. The more you demonstrate that others within your organization and beyond have helped to shape the outcome and are completely committed to it, the more others will buy in. Remember the point on community: it's not about you, it's about *us*. Best to let others take the stage and do the talking. Go all in on *all for one and one for all.*

Engagement motivates us. On the journey to achieve your particular outcome you cannot overcommunicate. Celebrate your successes. (Seriously. Celebrate them.) Keep everyone connected and informed, bringing them together physically and virtually as much as possible. The more everyone feels connected with one another and "in the know," the more powerful you collectively become.

Honesty motivates us. Openly acknowledge your setbacks, pulling from them the lessons learned and adjustments you've made. A plea in this regard: *do not* brush the bad under the rug. Acknowledge it, as it will teach you more than success ever will. It is real just like successes are, and everyone will understand and respect the unvarnished truth. Ask your community for feedback and act upon it. Remember that collectively you are as formidable as your community believes you are, and the wonderful reality is that *the truth in the building always becomes the truth on the street*. Always.

Progress motivates us. Do everything you can to show how you are advancing, as early and as often as possible. This is where sales results and other important metrics count and are hugely motivating, like the numbers on a scoreboard egging a team on toward victory.

BHAGs motivate us. These kind of stretch goals get humans nervous *and* excited. I've seen firsthand how setting sights higher than would be the natural trajectory—beyond probable, past possible, further on into unreasonable—unlocks bigger thinking that in turn makes bigger financial outcomes possible. Paraphrasing George Bernard Shaw, remember that progress, by its very nature, is unreasonable. Therefore, all progress depends upon unreasonable people. Aim higher. Watch how everyone steps up and figures out how to achieve the bigger bolder outcome.

And, lastly . . .

Say it plain. In strategy work of any kind it is always so tempting to go with "ten-dollar words" and business jargon, perhaps to make things sound more sophisticated and important. But here's the thing about unfamiliar or fancy terms: they have exactly the opposite effect on most people than what is intended. Rather than enhancing communication, they muddy it, with the result being confusion or even suspicion. Is there more hat here than cattle? Fancy words and technical jargon don't help your cause. Even when you're talking about complex things, there is always a way to say it plainly to ensure everyone can grasp your intentions.

16

The patient is on the table

The Old Navy story

LENN MURPHY HAD just come off a brilliant turn at Shoppers Drug Mart in Canada. Between 2001 and 2007, after a meteoric career at Loblaw Companies, he had become Chairman and CEO of Shoppers, quickly reset the strategy, and went on to create $10 billion in enterprise value in just six years. His success is the stuff of legend in Canadian retail. Due to a competitive restriction I could only watch the Shoppers transformation from the sidelines, yet everyone in the industry including me was riveted by the rapid retooling of the entire business: a reenergized and refocused leadership and culture, reimagined stores, entry into new categories and service offerings, stronger private brands, a turbo-charged loyalty program, and a reset of the entire go-to-market. It was a master class in reinvention. When Murphy left the business in 2007, I was hopeful he would land in a category without conflict and we could work together again. We had had a lot of fun together in the early Loblaw years working for John Lederer, and now here he was, a gifted transformational leader in his own right.

I needn't have worried. Within months of leaving Shoppers, Murphy's career took a surprising and opportune turn. Never shy of a challenge, he joined Gap Inc., as Chairman and CEO, taking on another business past its peak and in need of reinvention. This time, however, it was a category in which he had no experience, and the media was merciless ("Gap Names Glenn Murphy as CEO: Former Retail Exec Has No Apparel Experience," *Ad Age*, July 27, 2007). Not subtle, and not a small leap for even the most talented of retail leaders.

When Murphy and I reconnected, he had a very specific ask based upon my experience helping to create and market the apparel brand Joe Fresh, done in collaboration with Joe Mimran for the Loblaw organization. "Old Navy is the profit engine of Gap Inc., Joe, and it's first on my list to tackle.

Come to San Francisco and let's talk about how to get it firing again." On a beautiful late summer's morning, at the stately Gap headquarters on Folsom Street overlooking the Bay Bridge and the sparkling waters of the Pacific, I met Murphy to chat all things Old Navy. By sunset, in a cocktail bar, and after a few martinis together, I was working on the business.

The challenge with Old Navy was fourfold:

Firstly, the business had strayed from its core focus of casual clothing for families, chasing growth (and straining credibility) with offerings such as apparel for the office and day-into-night occasions.

Secondly, in a category it pretty much invented and had had to itself for years—namely cheap and cheerful clothing at a low price—it was now just one of many players, including Target, H&M, and Zara.

Thirdly, the brand, which had exploded on the scene with a California-lifestyle aesthetic (think board shorts, flip-flops, and graphic tees) and a fun, animated store experience, hadn't changed much in over a decade. As good as it was, the shine had all but faded.

Lastly, for a business that was fastest in U.S. retail history to reach a billion dollars in sales out of the gate, hitting that milestone at the four-year mark, Old Navy had subsequently experienced twenty consecutive quarters of decline. Ouch. That's a long run without good news, making reinvention and any kind of case for capital reinvestment doubly difficult. To say it was bad would be an understatement. I can recall Murphy informing a shocked internal audience at Old Navy headquarters in the Mission Bay district of San Francisco: "The patient is on the table and it's time to pull out the paddles." Murphy always had a way of putting things that got the blood flowing.

Here's what excited me about Old Navy: a cool brand, a little dusty but with good bones, with a disruptor's penchant for behaving differently. In some ways, already in its own category. I believed as Murphy did that it could be done, and it was a brilliant first move given that customers at all levels were trading down to value as a recession picked up force. A reinvigorated Old Navy could be a massive winner for Gap Inc.

Here's what freaked me out: He didn't just want a sharpened value proposition, a refreshed customer experience, and a sustained growth trajectory. He wanted sales to go up NOW. Like next quarter now, from negative momentum and at the start of the Great Recession. This was a big *hurry* audacious goal, the audacity of it believing that it could be done so quickly from such a low starting point.

It didn't take us long to figure out what we needed to do: *bring the fun back*. It was what customers said they loved most about the brand, in attitude, experience, and the products themselves. Nothing was too serious, and this happy easiness fit perfectly with low prices. In a way, Old Navy invented the kind of livable-and-not-so-precious-near-disposable-fashion that so many others caught onto, copied, and crowded the market with. And, fun was clearly in its DNA. Old Navy's early flagship stores had mechanical waist-down mannequins continuously high kicking to show off its denim assortment. Toy trains tooted and circled high above shoppers' heads on suspended tracks. Its mascot dog, Magic, conducted mock fashion shows in TV commercials with the actress Morgan Fairchild providing color commentary. Fun? Heck yeah! From the outset the brand was campy and completely magnetic to kids, teens, and parents—the trifecta of retail marketing.

By the time I arrived, though, fun had clearly left the building. Head office had a tense and demoralized vibe, something the newly appointed Old Navy President, Tom Wyatt, with his sunny Southern disposition and energy, was determined to fix. Store associates were scratching their heads over the arrival of wave after wave of products closer in aesthetic to the stylish, fast fashion brands like H&M than the casual fun clothes that made Old Navy famous. The store concept that had blown everyone away in 1994 had been left too long without a refresh, a reminder that thirteen years in retail is an eternity. The latest store prototype, opened just prior to Murphy's arrival, was expensive, strangely slick, and destined to never be replicated. In short, the case for change at Old Navy wrote itself, and at the helm was a self-confessed action junkie—Murphy—focused on immediate results.

In the weeks that followed, we tapped Crispin Porter Bogusky as our agency, with Alex Bogusky and Andrew Keller becoming our partners in crime. We galvanized our strategy around *fashion fun for all, and value is part of the fun,* essentially a return to the unique "category of one" position the brand had occupied and to where every data point was telling us to return. Combined with a financial BHAG centered on aggressive EBITDA growth, it was now time to roll up our sleeves. The merchant team focused first on the core offering of jeans, and together we developed a new architecture, or framework, for style, fit, naming, and brand expression, ultimately setting up that core category for growth. We set about creating a new brand for the exploding fitness apparel market, Old Navy's $29 antidote to the $100+ yoga pants craze going on across America. Most importantly, the merchants exited the office workwear category and whatever else that wasn't Old Navy, and instead focused on updating the brand-defining classics, from flip-flops (new colors) and cute summer dresses (fresh styles and patterns) to sweats and T-shirts (new cuts, fabrics, and graphics), and introduced new products that fit with the fun, family lifestyle. Base camp one on our climb.

Simultaneously, the internal marketing team and agency began building out a plan to re-message the brand. When we saw the first glimpses of what would become the Super Modelquins campaign, the creation of a family of super model–like mannequin characters to represent Old Navy, we were excited and could see the potential in these fresh new faces of fun. Not only would a family of plastic characters appear in TV spots and circulars, they would also physically "live" at the front of the stores as full-size mannequins, the stars of a serialized story that would unfold weekly in poses and outfits. This was breakthrough creative integration between store, print, digital, and airwaves. But all of it rested on finding a manufacturing company that could create and produce mannequins for over a thousand stores within a few months before relaunch. I will never forget reviewing, on an insanely tight deadline, endless variations of facial expressions we were about to give life to. If you live long enough, you get to experience absolutely everything.

Next up was a new store model. Even in an age of ecommerce it was decided that Old Navy's competitive advantage was the physical manifestation of its brand. We therefore needed a brand-defining store, a complete reimagination of what the future of the brand looked like. Specifically, we needed to address how the stores would once again become completely and magnetically fun. Old Navy first did it with props and animation and a wonderfully crazy, retro brand voice. No doubt that could work again if we did it in a fresh way. But our strategy was calling on us to go deeper than that, to *live fun* in absolutely everything we did, not just in how we looked and what we said. So, we asked ourselves the core question: What exactly is fun, anyway? Here's what we discovered:

> **Fun is surprising.**
> **Fun is visual playfulness and wordplay.**
> **Fun is getting more than you expected.**
> **Fun is what happens when we're together. In other words, fun is _human energy_.**

Bull's-eye. As we walked the stores we couldn't help noticing where energy lived. Real energy, the kind that generates an energized vibe that excites people, is *generated by people themselves*. The more concentrated they are the more energy they generate, and the more fun things become. (Ever notice how the best bars are always crowded? It's by design.) Where was the human energy in an Old Navy? At the front of the store in the check-out queue, where all that stuff was being purchased for so little money. At the back of the store near the changerooms, with all the buzzy comings and goings of people and product. And at peak shopping moments, in pockets throughout the store like denim and the kids' area. What would happen if we brought these experiences closer together, toward the center of the store? With the strategic outcome of *fashion fun for all, and value is part of the fun* running through our minds, we posed that question at an impromptu creative session in Las Vegas, in a dusty new store construction site we were touring at the time. Murphy, Wyatt, Craig Trettau (Director of Store Design at Gap and seconded to work on Old Navy), and I gathered around a makeshift drawing table, drawing and redrawing a diagram on a sheet of tracing paper, until we collectively said, "That's it!" Back we raced to the Mission Bay design studio to build scale model after scale model of a bold new store concept, built entirely from foam core, wire, and color printer outputs, and all designed to amplify fun. Murphy and Wyatt blessed it, and we now had a new model store on its way to testing in two San Francisco–area locations.

But we were still months away from bringing all of this to market, sales were still lagging, brand scores and morale continued to erode, and our impatient leader was still asking the same question. "When do I get my sales lift?" Rachel Acheson and her colleagues in internal marketing came back with something truly fun. What if we exploded a series of one-day promotional offers to wake up the market and drive retrial in the interim? That is exactly what we did, with iconic brand items at prices so low the police regularly had to be called for crowd control at shopping centers across America. Classic Old Navy flip-flops? $1. Ribbed tank tops in your choice of fabulous colors? $2. Your choice of denim? $12. A holiday sale for a holiday you've never heard of? We made it up, but no matter. Come one, come all, but come soon, as this stuff won't last! And they did. And so did sales, which fueled the reinvention with what I called "first fast steps." *Bang. Bang. Bang.* Murphy got his paddles and the patient popped back to life.

A little more than eighteen months from Glenn Murphy's arrival at Gap Inc., Old Navy was relaunched with the introduction of the Super Modelquins campaign, a massive return to national television supported by print and outdoor, and a PR and social media blitz that revealed paparazzi-style glimpses of the plastic model family partying with real-life celebs, lunching at the toniest of restaurants, and hanging at the beach (Super Modelquins—They're Just Like Us!) The brand image had been refreshed, as had its voice and messaging, just as the first waves of new product were reaching the stores. The store associates, once again free to sport tattoos and be themselves, injected the kind of people-energy back into the business that customers could feel and get swept up by. Sales moved from mid-single-digit negative to single-digit positive chainwide for the first time in five years. The new model stores? They jumped out of the gate in the mid-single digits and climbed to a performance lift in the high teens as the new campaign broke. Oh, and that yoga pant brand I mentioned? It became a $200 million business within a few short years. Murphy and the Board gave a green light to capitalizing an aggressive, market-by-market store renovation program, and the cash machine of Gap Inc. was once again dispensing money. With Old Navy reignited, and improvements beginning at Banana Republic and Gap, and the acquisitions of Athleta and Intermix, the share price of Gap Inc. went from ~$10 in 2009 to ~$50 when Murphy announced his retirement in late 2014. The key to all of this? A clear short- and long-term outcome we could picture and drive toward, something we obsessed over until it was achieved and then some. Now that is what I call fun.

17

Fifth Mindset Principle

Make Momentum Together

BODY AT REST tends to stay at rest. A body in motion tends to stay in motion. It is Newton's First Law of Motion, which dictates that unless an outside force acts upon something at rest, it is likely to stay that way. The follow-on point is that it takes a lot more energy to get a body in motion than to sustain it once it is.

It won't surprise you to hear that these rules apply to humans. Our natural instinct is to stay at rest to conserve energy. Unless we see something we absolutely must have (*Mmmm, I'm hungry and that looks appetizing so I'm going to chase it*) or we are threatened (*Yikes, I'm out of here!*) we are likely to stay put and keep watch.

When it comes to business, the same rules apply. Without a reason to move and evolve—either a compelling growth opportunity to pursue, or a threat that catalyzes change (e.g., new or intensifying competition, say, or a market shift)—the natural state is inertia. Not to the extent of complete inaction perhaps, but certainly toward what we might refer to as *business as usual*. Why change when we don't have to? It's that status quo thing again, and our natural bias toward it. What we really need is to be and remain in motion. What we really need on our side is *momentum*.

You may recall the formula from high school physics class: Momentum = Mass × Velocity. Simply explained, the greater the mass and the faster it is moving, the more momentum is created. It's a straight shot to apply this to reinvention: the more change you put into motion (a massing up of cohesive actions you are taking, hence the term "critical mass"), and the faster you go in implementing them (everyone on your team aligned, acting in unison and at a pace), the more momentum you are able to generate. Let's not forget how valuable momentum is. If you lead businesses and have been around awhile you already know what it's like when you have that force on your side, and what it's like when you don't. But beyond the fact that momentum helps a business in the normal run of things, it's even more important in a transformational context. Momentum is what enables a business to actually *stay in motion and sustain its own renewal*.

This is where businesses differ from inanimate objects. With objects, external forces influence their relative state. But with companies made up of people, it is both external *and* internal forces that influence their state and fate. If all those opposed to change within an organization wish to stop it, they can and will. That's how it is with unexpected change. Every organization has a built-in cultural defense system set to prevent bad things from happening, something akin to how white blood cells mobilize within a human body to eliminate threats. Momentum is the antidote, as it is the irrepressible force able to overcome them.

I recall a mid-level executive from Walgreens saying to me quietly in a hallway in Deerfield, Illinois, "I know you are here to change things, Joe, and I respect that. Just know that if we don't like what you're doing we'll stop it one way or another. Remember, we will be here long after you are gone." Fair point, one delivered honestly and with the best of intentions to an external change agent (literally, in my case, as a Canadian, a foreign body introduced into the system). Change gets stopped for many reasons. You can't blame people for concluding it's better not to take risk unless you help them to understand the greater risk is in not changing. And, you can't blame them for feeling like stuff is about to be done to them unless you demonstrate you're going to do it together.

Here's how to *Make Momentum Together*:

Consult widely (and be seen to consult widely). Ask your people what they think. Share with them what you think, and what you are uncovering. Tell them the truth. As things develop, poll them to get their feedback. I can guarantee that on the day you stand on a stage to share in detail where you are going, and you ask for their full and tireless support to get there, you will be doubly glad you did.

Make no plans alone. If you are a leader of a team, then play as one. Do strategy with *all* of your direct reports, and do it collaboratively. It cannot be your strategy. It must be *our strategy*. Then replace the idea of a strategy *cascade*, the communication down to lower levels, with a more productive approach: strategy *engagement*. As you share the details with the next level down—those who truly hold the levers in their hands—tell them genuinely this is a DRAFT strategy and plan, and before it is finalized you need them to engage with it, work through how they will execute it, make it better if possible, and then get behind it to bring it to life. It will only get better and the buy-in will only go up.

One team and one way forward. Success is what happens *after* a strategy is complete and launched. Yet so many leaders launch it and leave it. Don't. Stay with it. Tie everything back to it. Measure all progress against it and keep the feedback loop alive. As Bill Durnan, my first Chief Creative Officer and collaborator on reinvention in the early days, would say, "If you want to chop down a giant tree, it's best to keep hitting it in the same spot again and again and again." When you apply the force that comes from working as a sharply focused team, you'll get through it in no time.

Go as fast as you possibly can. This is a straight build from Create the Future Now. The benefit of moving quickly? As we like to say north of the 49th parallel, you get a "twofer": action begets action (remember the velocity part of the formula for momentum) and speed generates both excitement and followers.

Overcommunicate. Share and keep sharing. People like to know where they stand. They value being reminded of the plan and hearing of progress. They also like to hear from you, from their leaders, and see you fighting the good fight, too. It gives them confidence and helps them find the strength to press on when the going gets tough. In transformational times it pays to be visible. Just about the worst thing you can do is to be absent or leave people guessing. Humans naturally conclude the worst unless they hear otherwise. Tell the story as it unfolds, keep telling it, and ask your teammates to do the same.

18

I do
(until I don't)

The David's
Bridal story

THOUGHT WEDDINGS WERE supposed to be celebratory affairs, intended to leave everyone with a lifetime of happy memories. Right? Not so in the case of my commercial marriage with David's Bridal. With all its promise and good intentions at the outset, it was a complete and absolute bust. All that remains are signatures on a worthless piece of paper, painful memories, and a few hard lessons learned. Without overdramatizing (likely too late I suppose, but what are weddings without a little drama?), I still ask myself to this day, *What went wrong?* I still hold on to the belief that things could have turned out differently, if only.

But this much I do know. Firstly, I co-own the outcome, as I fully subscribe to the notion that almost nothing is "done to us." Rather, we are most often at least co-authors of our own story and fate. In every reinvention I am an influencer and not a decision maker, yet that doesn't fully absolve me from sharing blame. There were moments when the courage to be sufficiently bold failed me. Secondly, regardless of how things first appear (in this case the perfect match wrapped in white lace and beckoning: a distressed business in need of reinvention, a private equity owner in search of a solution, a Reinventionist willing to engage and invest), it is wise to remember that change itself, no matter how attractive, is at once an ally and formidable foe. It can and will take you to bliss. It can and will knock you on your backside if you don't step up and stay with it. The difference rests on how you go about it.

There isn't a more emotionally engaging category in retail than the wedding business. Right there at the intersection of ancient religious tradition, where the union of two people has been held up as sacred for centuries, and modern consumer marketing, elevating expectations, and manufacturing desire, the wedding has few rivals when it comes to rituals rich with emotions. It doesn't matter who you are, which culture raised you, how old you are, or even how much money you have. When it comes to weddings there is one universal truth: everything... must... be... PERFECT. Or as perfect as humanly possible. The ring. The invitations. The venue. The table setting and decorations. The carriage or town car that whisks the bride and groom away. And, of all the perfect everythings, the most important of these is this: THE DRESS. In the bride's mind, in that shining moment, it is her dress that symbolizes the institution of marriage and her commitment to it. The dress does the talking for her. The dress embodies what she wishes to say to friends, family, and her many followers on Instagram. It speaks volumes. "I am happy and content." "This union is perfect." "Everything going forward will be perfect." This is what we uncovered. Young or old, highly or minimally educated, well-heeled or just well-accustomed to getting by on a budget, in every case the dream was the same. Let it be *perfect*. Let it be unique and mine alone. And, let it be as aspirational *and* affordable as possible.

Right there. That's the spot where David's Bridal shone the brightest.

Picking the perfect dress is a complicated affair. While things like fit and silhouette are important, the decision is ultimately made on how narrow the gap is between the picture in a bride's head and the money in her purse. While this dynamic exists broadly in all of fashion, it is acutely true in bridal. In America today, that dream-within-reach desire translates into a bridal industry worth $72 billion annually, $3 billion of which is spent on dresses. For decades, David's Bridal sold about a third of them. Given that the average price for a wedding dress in America is $1,700, 68 percent of brides surveyed said they spent less than $1,000, and the average sale at David's Bridal was closer to $600, that's one heck of a lot of dresses.

Beginning with a single store in Fort Lauderdale, Florida, in 1950, David's Bridal grew faster than a wedding guest list. By the turn into this century it had expanded to all fifty states and secured its position as the go-to destination for value, one of the first retail "category killers." On any given Saturday the fitting rooms were packed, and the buzz of brides and bridesmaids was deafening. I can remember a former colleague of mine, David Saffer, who had helped the company with customer research work in the early 2000s, describe the brand in loving terms, "David's Bridal is a beautiful thing. It sells desire with the simplest of messages: *The dream is real, and you can afford it.*" With the near-perfect formula for success, selling reasonable facsimiles of the dream from "$99! Limited time!" and up, the entire business was built on pulling in the aspiring bride with the promise of the perfect dress at an affordable price; then, upselling and "group selling" its way to a bigger purchase. A little nicer dress, all the essential accessories, and, of course, gowns for the bridesmaids, too. In stores from Annapolis to Wichita, David's Bridal was packed from morning to night with group appointments in full pursuit of perfection.

Of course, all of this was before the big discounters like Target and H&M entered the category, focused on taking shares at the price/value end of the market. This was before mid-level merchandise players like J.Crew and Ann Taylor jumped in, chasing growth from the other end of the value spectrum by bringing higher-quality fabrics and style within reach of the average budget, well below the high price points of the independent bridal boutiques where the majority of the sales volume lived. This was before younger brides, all digital natives, began building inspiration boards on Pinterest (close to 60 percent of brides start there) and clicking through theknot.com, an out-of-nowhere phenomenon bringing content to an inspiration-hungry community of brides, not only expanding their horizons on what to buy but *from whom.* Before these same young people began delaying their wedding plans, staying single longer than prior consumer cohorts. Each of these shifts and incursions pulled at the threads of the company's oversized hold on the wedding gown market. Each served up yet another illustration of how the world has a way of shifting around those with the most to lose, and how those with the most to lose have a habit of turning a blind eye to it.

Now, a challenged business is one thing, but a bankrupt one is quite another. While there was a robust case for change to be made and the need for speed to do something in 2010, the business was not dead by any measure. Like much of legacy retail at that moment, it had yet to get serious about digital. It hadn't yet grasped how this dimension of customer experience would become the real battlefield on which to win. While stores still had a vital role to play, the customer's journey was increasingly beginning and ending digitally. The business had also missed or ignored key trends such as the casualization of weddings. What we now know as the classic and standard "bride in white" was a postwar creation. Previously, brides wore their best dress, whatever it was they felt made them look their best. Beginning in the mid-2000s there was a return to that notion, plus a growing pivot toward informality—what you might call today the Free People or Anthropologie wedding style. A sizeable portion of today's brides reject the idea of a white dress entirely (approximately 11 percent and growing) in favor of the consciously imperfect alternative. Worse, growth was no longer in the discount end of the market—this was actually shrinking along with the number of weddings held annually. Rather, growth was mostly in what might be described as the "affordable luxury" segment. There was still a place and role for opening price-point dresses, but the price-conscious bride was increasingly inclined to trade up. They wanted what the stars were wearing, or as close as they could get to the look of a Kate or Victoria or Beyoncé.

That was the position David's Bridal was in at the start of reinvention. With close to 30 percent market share, it was defying gravity while surrounded by big discounters on one end and upstart players on the other. It was attempting to stay true to its model of the white-dress-for-less in all its variations, yet with each passing year it looked a little more frayed and a little more out of touch with the times.

Yet none of this was particularly dire or daunting; save for a nuance here or there, this is what the transformation of most sixty-year-old businesses looks like at the beginning. I was actually pretty bullish, as, up until that point, I had been batting a thousand in retail reinvention. With a deal in place, my team and I got busy doing what we do: immersing ourselves in the business and the current customer experience; talking with executives, frontline associates, and customers; gathering and analyzing every bit of data we could get our hands on; digging deep into the backstory and DNA of the brand. Through it all, we sought the kind of insights upon which leadership could build a strategy and stage a transformation, and we found plenty.

For example, brides weren't seeking only the dress ending in a transaction, they were seeking a supportive relationship that would yield an emotional benefit: there was a lot of money attached to achieving that. In a mass-market world of homogenous choices and experiences, brides wanted to feel it was uniquely all about them.

It wasn't just the big details that mattered to brides; for example, a wide range of styles to choose from, but the smallest of details. How they felt about the seamstress charged with their perfect fitting was a massive value-creation moment, never mind stress reliever.

Armed with these insights and more, and with a very granular sense of where the money was, we collaborated with leadership to make the most important choices: which customers to focus on; how we would win with them; what our purpose and position as a brand were, staying true to our DNA yet making it resonant for today; and finally, how we would bring these choices to life in the most compelling end-to-end customer experience. Within eighteen weeks we knew exactly where to go and how to get there, the Board was aligned, and we were on our way. Better still, within a few months we began to see the first evidence in field that we were on the right track. Perfect.

Then, like a cheap dress in the rain, everything came apart.

Regardless of whether the executives, who together with my team had shaped strategy; or private equity ownership, who had pressure tested our convictions and blessed it; for different reasons—some openly shared and some behind the scenes—alignment became misalignment; clarity gave way to second-guessing and alternative strategies; unity gave way to factions and fragmentation. Executives were replaced, and new ones arrived with their own ideas and allegiances. From start to finish, the leadership team was entirely replaced. Save for the Board, not one executive was there through it all. As a result, what was once "our strategy" increasingly became "your strategy." Proof that we were on the right track was no longer being actively sought and celebrated; the opposite pursuit became the norm. Wherever there was opportunity to show how strategy was flawed or executions sub-par, it was amplified. And as the execution of strategy continued to unfold, the field was sent mixed signals, as were customers, until no one had any idea what David's Bridal stood for anymore. Was it the reliable and cheap wedding dress depot? Or the "designer dresses for less" destination? Was it the source for inspiration, or the place to go once a bride knew what she wanted? Was it a transactional experience or an emotionally rewarding one? The answer depended upon who was asked the question.

There is only one thing worse than no strategy, and that is many strategies at once. On any given day one direction would be given, only to have it countered the next. Person by person, piece by piece, what was once a clear and "all-in" action plan broke down into an "everyone for themselves" free-for-all. It got so bad that at one point I asked for a regroup in New York, away from head office, where the entire senior team could gather to review and realign on strategy. One strategy. Our collective strategy. I recall making an impassioned case for why attempting to ride several horses at one time was a really bad idea, and literally asked everyone to pledge their commitment to a single strategy. Everyone responded with "I do!" We even memorialized the moment by snapping a photo of us all, hands clasped and raised, ready to roll together once again with a unified way forward.

But in the days that followed the change-outs and side conversations continued. Multiple strategies were kept alive on the basis of "I am an expert in this area, and I was brought into fix it, so I'm going to do it my way." A few weeks after that meeting, a late-joining executive presented a wholly new conceptualization of the brand image than the one we had all collaborated on for months. It was approved without so much as a regroup, and the last vestiges of unity were lost.

Against a backdrop of market forces continuing to gain strength, and brides increasingly growing used to digitally-led ways of engagement that didn't lead to the door of David's Bridal, what was once a slow-drip decline became a torrent. Whether or not the strategy was sound, and many believed it was, as I did, it never stood a chance. The true power of any strategy lies in the collective will of those who believe in it and see it through. As I've learned, full-on execution of a good strategy beats lackluster execution of a great one every time.

Suffice it to say David's Bridal for me was a painful experience, yet rich with insights and a silver lining. In this case, it was two big lessons:

Firstly, before proceeding with reinvention, it's wise to fully assess whether the conditions for success are there at the outset. Give thought to whether fundamental enablers—things like leadership, talent, wherewithal, and will—are in place (I will talk more about this in chapters twenty-one and twenty-two). In my excitement to engage and get going I didn't fully consider the question I was asked, "Should we wait until we have a new CEO in place before we begin?"

Secondly, in any kind of transformation you either align and make momentum together, or you fail. There is no equivocating on this point. I saw what was happening firsthand, and I did try to do something about it. Yet, eventually I threw up my hands in exasperation and hoped somehow it would all miraculously work out. Mistake. There are no miracles in reinvention, only sharp focus, collective agreement, and relentless effort. Given that the future of the business was on the line—not to mention our collective reputations and investment—I should not have rested until those with decision-rights addressed the issue head on. Or, I should have been fired trying. The formula is quite simple: pick a lane, commit to it, stick together, and never waver from the course come what may. In reinvention, no one single misstep is ever a fail, only an opportunity to learn, adjust, firm up your footing, and move forward. Never ever stop until you have achieved your collective outcome. For a number of reasons, none of this happened. We didn't Make Momentum Together, and that's the lesson of the story. Sadly, my commercial bride and I will take it to our graves rather than the bank.

19

Again, but differently this time

The JCPenney story

T HE PHONE CALL presaged the news articles by about a minute. On the other end of the phone was Jill Soltau, then CEO of Joann Stores, a business my team and I had had an incredible run helping to reinvent. As we were still engaged with Joann, I presumed the call was to touch base on several follow-on initiatives. Yet it turned out Soltau wasn't calling about that. She simply shared she was leaving Joann and that it would be announced shortly that she would be in a new position at a different company. Momentarily as it turned out.

The story topped the morning's business news headlines: Jill Soltau announced as JCPenney's next CEO. Big news for a storied retailer fallen on hard times and without a Chief Executive since the unexpected departure of Marvin Ellison, in June of 2018.

In what must have been the blurriest of transitory moments, I could tell Soltau was already moving ahead at full speed. She explained how difficult it was to leave Joann at a time when all the heavy lifting was beginning to pay off and the future was bright. But in the end, JCPenney was the kind of opportunity a career retailer, merchant, and now-seasoned transformational leader couldn't pass up. Here was an iconic retail institution on the heels of several unsuccessful attempts at reinvention, yet still beloved and very much part of the fabric of life in America. If there was a dare-to-be-great opportunity in retail, this was it, and there was a positive consensus forming on the news of her appointment. "Jill Soltau Is a Winning Choice as the New CEO of JCPenney" (*Forbes*, October 2018).

The news got me thinking about JCPenney in the Ron Johnson years (CEO from 2011 to 2013), specifically about what went wrong. Now, with someone I knew and admired at the helm, I returned to the story to understand it more fully. To see what was there to be gleaned from a much-publicized yet failed reinvention. As I wasn't involved, this meant reading everything I could find on it—mostly media interviews and expert analysis—and piecing it together as best I could.

JCPenney is an approximately 850-store giant with millions of square feet of selling space, much of it in malls across America. Through much of the last decade, and through several high-profile attempts at resetting the company for growth, the business had, despite its size and reach, not been able to find a sustainable groove. It continued to lose share in key categories like women's apparel, and when it was mentioned in the media it was often in the context of continued poor performance and the increasing irrelevance of the department store model. The fundamental question wasn't only whether it could be fixed ("Killing JCPenney: Can the Iconic Retailer Be Saved?" *Forbes*, July 2018), it was whether there was still a place in the world at all for a "mid-market department store." In an era of strong discount department stores (Kohl's), hard discount general merchants (Target, Walmart), evergreen discount apparel players (Old Navy), fast fashion houses (H&M), outlet models (Nordstrom Rack), and the new model "everything store" (Amazon), plus all the sales promotion that had become the new normal (a stunning fact: over 75 percent of all apparel in America is now sold below regular price), many concluded it would not be possible for JCPenney to secure a defensible and profitable position again. The closest reference point was Macy's, a notch or two above JCPenney in terms of price/quality, yet a similar model, whose own reinvention continues to be a hard climb with mixed results. The other unfortunate reference was Sears.

With these factors considered—competitive intensity and disruption, continued weak performance, uncertainty about the future of the department store model itself, and questions circling about the role of physical stores in an era of online shopping growth—the company's stock price was floating at historically low levels, narrowing further its wherewithal to make substantial moves.

Any question of *Could it be saved?* was heavily complicated by the related question, *Why hadn't it worked previously?* JCPenney in the Ron Johnson era wasn't just a fail. It was a massive fail, on a scale unseen before. According to *Forbes*, "The Johnson era at JCPenney will go down in history as one of the most destructive reigns by any CEO in any company—ever... In 2012, at the end of Johnson's first year as CEO, same-store sales fell 25 percent resulting in a $4.3 billion decrease in revenue." Everything since that point, under the leadership of successor Ellison, appeared to have been a lightning-fast retreat to the perceived safety of the past before Johnson. That plan hadn't worked well either, but at least it wasn't as dramatically unsuccessful and costly.

As I dove further into JCPenney's recent past, and thought more about why strategies fail, a thesis began to develop in my mind. Let's call it the *twin paradox of failed strategies* thesis, which goes like this:

Paradox one: First, and most obviously, companies that are in most need of reinvention are those in the worst position to engineer one (Staples is a good example, prior to its acquisition by Sycamore). The longer it goes, and the greater the need, the harder it gets. All by itself, this is the strongest argument in favor of reinventing before you are forced to.

Paradox two: The more desperate the circumstances, the bolder the actions required to change the trajectory. But the truly bold course is the riskier one; therefore, de-risking bold moves, *while continuing to be bold*, becomes central. It becomes THE success factor.

Johnson's strategy was indeed bold. Reverse engineering it, I would describe it as follows:

1   As much as possible, shift to more unique and exclusive offerings, and in this case a greater weighting toward national brands (as compared to "own" or private brands, which were a core strength of the business).

2   Create a differentiated experience around those offerings ("dozens of in-store boutiques surrounding a town square" was the concept) and a cachet around the JCPenney brand itself.

3   Move to everyday low pricing, getting off the high/low promotional heroin that was apparently sucking the life out of margins and the business.

4   Package it all up with a fresh brand image, with updated, easier-to-shop stores and supporting communications, and take it all to market quickly and with a bang.

The surprise? It quite possibly might have worked. Much of points one, two, and four above are essentially today's retail playbook on how to survive in the Amazon era: sell customers what they can't get anyplace else (with a nod here to marketing and the art of creating desire), deliver an omni-channel experience that makes it magnetic, and get as close to the benchmark of "easy" as humanly possible.

What virtually guaranteed the strategy wouldn't work, however, was how it was executed. This was the true point of failure in my view. Going back to the twin paradox theory, a bold strategy was clearly called for. Check. Yet it wasn't de-risked and therefore had almost no chance at success, meaning:

1   They made a hard-and-fast cut from old to new, without full buy-in of employees, most critically customer-facing associates. I knew this firsthand, as at the time I popped into a store to get a sense of what was new and different under Johnson, and a two-minute conversation with a sales associate made everything clear: "I really don't understand what management is thinking these days. All I know is I have a bunch of angry customers to deal with and they're not coming back." She was clearly not onside, and neither were customers.

2   Those long-standing customers had essentially been fired; customers who had become accustomed to buying only when items were on sale. When they weren't on sale as often or as deeply, they just stopped buying as often or as much. There was also an overt push toward attracting younger customers in a hurry, although the customer base tended to be older.

3   From everything I have read and gathered, they appear to have done it in command-and-control style, with orders from the top cascading to those below without explanation or room for input.

I fully acknowledge my assessment is after the fact, and influenced by media and expert consensus, almost all of which concluded the strategy was wrong and, given the results, not particularly favorable. Still, it's worth asking, *What if?*

What if employees had understood and bought into the "why" of it all? If only they had seen change as a good and necessary thing, something they were part of rather than it "being done to them."

What if there had been a deeper understanding of who customers really were and what they wanted, rather than a broad bias toward younger customers led by demographics and not mindset?

What if customers had had the opportunity to migrate from what they were familiar with and the time to fall in love with what was new and different rather than being forced to make a hard trade?

What if the national brands and manufacturers had felt more like partners and less like vendors? (There was huge outcry from this community, such an incredibly important success factor in transformation.)

What if changes had been made on a *prove and move* basis, building more and more momentum, piece by transformative piece, instead of trying to flip a switch from old to new?

What if.

The only thing I know for certain is that the Johnson transformation didn't work. Yet it might have. There are no stats available on how many companies embark on new strategies and fail. But in the many that I have studied, I do see a pattern. Strategies, particularly those in transformational situations, fail for three readily apparent reasons:

1   They are flawed strategies.
2   They are sound strategies, yet factors beyond control cause them to fail.
3   They are sound strategies, conditions are right, yet they fail due to lack of buy-in, cohesive follow-through, or both.

The first two are obvious: it was the wrong strategy (e.g., BlackBerry), or a sound strategy up to a point brought to its knees by unforeseen forces (e.g., Blockbuster and the rise of delivery and then digital streaming). The third reason, lack of buy-in, is worth probing more deeply, as it is the most common. Why? Why does an arguably sound strategy fail? For one easily avoidable reason: *strategies are shaped in isolation, forced onto organizations, and therefore people don't see them as their own.*

Typically, most strategies are crafted by a few top leaders who set goals and devise a strategy to achieve them, often with the help of management consultants. Eventually others are brought into the process, but usually it is a small team exercise, with, therefore, a small subset of the full leadership team co-owning strategy. Functional leaders are brought in on a subject matter basis, usually only when detailed plan development is required. The broader organization is not engaged until they are told where to go and what to do.

On some level it makes sense as a classic inner circle, militaristic/command-and-control scenario, with decision making tightly held at the top and cascading down on a need-to-know basis. Unfortunately, it is the root cause of why strategies fail:

> **Humans tend to support that which they help create, and resist that which is forced upon them.**

Conversely, people will work harder and faster to get to a place they are excited about and feel they had a hand in choosing and defining. Which would you choose?

My conclusion is that this is what happened at JCPenney in the Johnson years, in the extreme. Strategy was "told through" rather than collaboratively shaped and therefore "sold through." It wasn't de-risked. De-risked by making a clear case for change. De-risked by having a compelling outcome and showing what was in it for everyone. De-risked by having everyone genuinely feel it was their strategy and therefore causing them to lean in hard to make momentum together. De-risked by effectively figuring it out and doing it together as a team. De-risked by a shared sense of ownership. When we do these things, the odds of any particular strategy being effective go up.

History, customers, and shareholders will ultimately be the judge of whether or not Jill Soltau and her team will be successful with the next leg of the JCPenney journey. Knowing Soltau from the Joann reinvention, I believe this time it will be done differently.

Do you have a strategy?

The idea of strategy was born in war times, "us versus them" conflicts dating back to early history and involving "a plan for military operations and movements during a war or battle." The term itself is derived from the Greek word for generalship or leading an army. When used in a business context it generally refers to "a plan of action or policy designed to achieve a major or overall aim."

Achieving a major aim is the main point. Leaders of all kinds have learned that to achieve substantial, often longer-term objectives, they are wise to have a strategy and think it through carefully. There is usually a lot riding on it. Things like growth and success (or decline and failure), the value of the business itself, the fortunes of those invested, and professional reputations. Surprising then that so many commercial strategies are built in the barest of ways: a collection of objectives and numbers, a tactical plan, and marching orders. All logic and no lore and love. This full-logic approach may seemingly work for war, but consider that in conflict the emotional dimensions are built in. What may appear on the surface to be top-down, command-and-control execution of rational strategies would miss the very human and emotionally charged dimensions that motivate armies to fight harder when the going gets tough. Things like fighting for personal freedom and the love of country. Or protecting a set of ideals from an enemy bound to destroy them. Or simply not dying. At some basic human level this emotional content is baked into every military strategy in history, and armies throughout history have been motivated by it. The deepest of human reasons for battling on when barriers and hardship come, as they always do, were there. So how is it that business strategy ended up being so deadly dull? All numbers and no point. How did we (and do we) accept the all-rational version and treat it as standard issue, continuing to pass it off as real and full strategy?

As business leaders we continue to do so at our peril. Strategies fail for many reasons but chief amongst them is a lack of buy-in and follow-through. In transformational situations the odds of failure are much higher, as these are closer in nature to extended, multi-front battles than what would be considered normal course business. Let's understand and accept that, in business as in war, *strategies do not win battles, people do.* It would follow that successful strategies are framed in ways that people can get excited about, and are based upon insights people can grasp, relate to, and align with. Ask American soldiers if they believe in the ideals of America, and whether this motivates them. Strategy is not a rational exercise alone.

For all these reasons, here is the definition of strategy I penned and work with every day:

Strategy is the high-level human how of achieving a sustainably advantageous position together with a robust financial outcome. It becomes strategy only with full organizational alignment and execution.

In other words, you don't actually have a strategy until everyone buys into and is acting on it. By this definition, do you have one?

You're almost there, with one last story to go.

To me there is a certain symmetry in making the story of Duane Reade's reinvention the last, as it was the first I signed up for after leaving Loblaw Companies, the one that formally kicked off my journey to Reinventionist.

As we wrapped up our work on Duane Reade and were preparing to leave New York, I recall John Lederer—at that moment, outgoing CEO of Duane Reade—saying to me:

"Something tells me, Joe, that this gig will forever change the way we work and think."

He was right. It did.

20

Faster than a New York minute

The Duane Reade story

WALK THE STREETS of Manhattan, from Battery Park to the Bronx, from the West Side Highway to the East River. If you're observant you'll take note of three things: First, neighborhoods are not defined by neat borders but by traffic; two sides of a busy avenue might as well be a continent apart when it comes to daily routines. Next, regardless of which neighborhood they call home, most everything Manhattanites consume on a daily basis is sourced within a few blocks of where they live. Lastly, the population of Manhattan more than doubles during the workday, so life between 7 a.m. and 7 p.m. is as close to a pitched battle for time and efficiency as you will find anywhere on the planet. Manhattan is not an easy place to live, and the boroughs aren't much easier.

Founded in 1960, Duane Reade was barely a drugstore, with a pharmacy counter added in the late seventies to capture more share of wallet from the surrounding blocks. Yet that was its particular appeal: it had *everything* New Yorkers could possibly need, matched to the particular complexion of each "micro hood" and its citizens. No two stores were alike in their offerings or footprint, which was noteworthy in an era when every chain retail store was a cookie-cutter replica of the original. Duane Reade had a shape-shifting ability to insinuate itself into every conceivable configuration of recycled city real estate and make a highly localized go of it. Twenty-five hundred square feet or twenty thousand. One floor, two, or even three. Long and narrow, or big and boxy. I recall standing in a tiny location wondering how on earth a patch of store the size of a New York hotel room could be productive. That was before I saw the obscured staircase and traveled upwards to discover what was once a movie theater, now full of thousands of square feet of stuff New Yorkers apparently needed. Compression stockings? Yep. Stocking stuffers? Uh-huh. Plush toys for a last-minute birthday gift? Check. Every possible type and texture of condom? Roger that. It really was quite astounding to tour the endless variety of Duane Reade stores and take note of their differences. Another memorable moment arrived deep in a basement beneath a store in lower Manhattan, at the very back of which was a dim and narrow hallway leading beneath the street above into a former coal storage room. "What the heck do you merchandise down there?" I jokingly asked on my first official walkabout. "Feminine hygiene and toilet paper," came the humorless reply, revealing the fascinating logic that shoppers were willing to work harder to locate these essential categories. It was explained to me this way: "You could put stuff in the back room. If New Yorkers need it, they'll dig it out." It's a tough city.

By the time I arrived on the scene, Duane Reade had spread to virtually every nook and cranny of the five NYC boroughs. Stores could be found everywhere, sometimes down the street or even around the corner from one another. The company's market share of pharmacy and drugstore-type merchandise, a key measure of competitive strength, had jumped to over 60 percent in Manhattan—a virtually unheard-of position in a dense and attractive market like New York—and over 30 percent share in the boroughs combined. Sales per square foot? Highest of drugstores in America. And the iconic Duane Reade shopping bag—ubiquitous on the streets of the city—was affectionately considered by notable New Yorkers as "urban luggage," the contents of which might include the manuscript of a famous author's book on a final journey to its publisher (true story). Duane Reade, named for two parallel streets crossing Broadway in Tribeca, was as much a part of the fabric and lore of daily life in New York as rushing yellow taxi cabs and the 840 miles of subway lines running beneath the surface.

For customers though, Duane Reade was a challenge. As the chain neared its fiftieth birthday, the red, white, and blue stores were in a sad state of disrepair. Aisles were cluttered. Shelves were crammed. Sales associates—legendarily surly—were beleaguered by low wages and high expectations. (The only thing tougher than shopping in a Duane Reade store was working in one.) It was not an uncommon occurrence to see actual fights between customers over who was next to check out, and duanereadesucks.blogspot.com was a popular website.

Oak Hill Capital Partners had purchased Duane Reade in 2004. After several years of block and tackling, led by then CEO Rick Dreiling and his Chief Operations Officer Chuck Newsome, solid retailers both, the business had been stabilized and many of the worst offenses—such as too much inventory and too little control of it—had been addressed. Yet it was still burdened with too much debt, sales were flagging, associate turnover was high, and customer satisfaction was at an all-time low. By the close of 2007, it was clear to the owners that they had no shot of achieving their original investment thesis (the high-level financial plan laid out when private equity purchases assets like Duane Reade). Worse, they were underwater on the original purchase price, meaning if they sold at that moment, they would get less than what they paid for it. Speculation was building in the tight-knit New York financial community that Oak Hill would be forced to write off their investment in Duane Reade and take a humbling loss. But to Tyler Wolfram, rising in the ranks of Oak Hill's partners and responsible for the day-to-day consumer and retail portfolio, failure wasn't an option. A tanking investment in Duane Reade—a pervasive presence and daily reminder to every financial player in New York—wasn't part of the plan. Dreiling was out, on his way to a spectacular leadership run at Dollar General, and a new leader would be named.

In April of 2008, John Lederer left his short-lived retirement to become the CEO of Duane Reade. Wolfram had wooed Lederer with a simple pitch: "Sure, it will be a challenge. No doubt about it. But it's a big opportunity and it's New York, so it will be fun." If ever there was a Canadian Mountie riding to the rescue, Lederer was it.

As fate would have it, just as Lederer was settling into his new digs in New York, I was figuring out my next gig after Loblaw. Lederer and I had kept in touch since our Loblaw days, and I was excited to see him step back into the ring. He was, and is, a huge talent, on a very short list of leaders I would follow into any battle. And for certain this would be an epic battle. Duane Reade, despite being the undisputed market leader, was at the time defying gravity and had no place to go but down. The big national drugstore chains—Walgreens, CVS, Rite Aid—were coming at the market fast, renovating and opening new stores at a pace. Worse, once we had data, we could see how Duane Reade was trailing far behind its rivals in every measure customers cared about. The sobering truth was this: New Yorkers would jump at any viable alternative, and the big, shiny, national network alternatives were pouring into the market. As I said to *Bloomberg Businessweek* some years later, "We knew that without bold and immediate action we were history. The only thing we couldn't predict was when we would be killed."

Have you heard how hot it can get in New York City in summer? Whatever you can imagine doesn't come close to the heat we felt that summer of 2008. On closer inspection, our starting point was much worse than we initially surmised (a complete data set has a way of making things abundantly clear). The competitive threat was greater and more imminent. The need for capital investment larger. The pressure to act was real, and time was a luxury we could not afford. On this point, Lederer, along with the stellar team he was assembling—Frank Scorpiniti, from Longs Drugs on the West Coast to run pharmacy; Joe Magnacca, from Shoppers Drug Mart in Canada, to lead Merchandising; Marc Saffer and Jim Scarfone, the only two New Yorkers on the team, leading IT and HR, respectively; Chuck Newsome, in the continued role of leading field operations; and me, leading strategy and brand transformation—were completely aligned. Exactly how to move forward was another matter up for vigorous debate.

In the exchange between the Cheshire Cat and Alice in Lewis Carroll's *Alice's Adventures in Wonderland,* Alice asked the Cheshire Cat, who was sitting in a tree, "What road do I take?" The cat inquired, "Where do you want to go?" "I don't know," Alice answered. "Then," said the cat, "it really doesn't matter." In the summer of 2008, feeling the intense heat and pressure to act fast, we had yet to define an outcome and craft a strategy to achieve it, therefore every road seemed like a viable option. My request of Lederer was to give us a few months to finish gathering the data, develop customer and competitive insights we could hang a strategy on, and get everyone aligned on where we're going and how we're going to get there. In other words, thoughtfully pick a lane. His reply would ultimately determine the fate of the business and, in a way, how I would forever think differently about shaping strategy and orchestrating change: "Take as much time as you need to get it right. But in the meantime, let's go on instinct and START DOING STUFF NOW." His expectations couldn't have been any clearer.

Though I came up through the ranks of the creative community, at heart I'm a strategist. And up to that point in my career I had learned the cardinal rule of strategy: Unless you want to mess around with style over substance, it's best to know where you're going before you start going there. It's a chess thing. Don't move until you see it, but when you see it, *move.* At that moment in 2008, I couldn't yet see it—the future of Duane Reade and its sustainable place in the retail order of things—yet my colleagues and I were being asked by Lederer (that's a polite way of characterizing it) to start making substantial moves. So that's what we did. While we began the work of figuring out where to play and, against long odds, how we could possibly win, we just started doing stuff in the meantime. The "stuff" fell into three buckets. First: quick wins, where we could get at immediate performance improvements without worrying too much about strategic value or competitive position. There were lots of these opportunities to be had. Second: we executed so-called tests and learns, where we would experiment with more ambitious changes that would hopefully reveal something valuable. Third: a hands-on reshaping of how we showed up, from the design of the stores and brand image to the way we packaged and messaged the content we had to work with at the outset. These were actions guided by feelings—instinct, intuition, experience, and judgment. Before we had a full set of facts to work with. Before the new private brands were launched. Before the product and category innovation. Before the new loyalty program. Before the operating model was retooled. Before we had a clearly defined outcome and a real strategy to get there. We simply took our best shot based on hypotheses, failed fast, and scaled anything that worked to buy us time.

Working in this way—on parallel tracks—we did something none of us could have predicted. We saw firsthand how action caused more action, manufacturing momentum while it fed insight, and "feel" for what was possible. If we had only taken action without the corresponding strategy development, we would have simply been throwing stuff at the wall with the hopes it would stick. If we had only carefully developed a strategic road map and then acted, all would have been lost. (By 2009, we had the added challenge of a full-blown recession!) Doing these things simultaneously, and keeping them tightly linked, let us leap forward out of the gate while we were figuring everything out and honing the navigation system to guide us. As we went, ever sharpening our course, we picked up speed to the point we became unstoppable. Not only did that give us an advantage, it energized the heck out of everyone.

Faster and faster we went. We reorganized test stores into three zones—How I Look, How I Feel, and What I Need Now—a more intuitive organizing principle that made sense for the customer and not just the business. We augmented and amplified the content we had to work with in ways that excited and resonated with customers. Who knew that

"Men's Grooming," for example, would become a huge thing a few years later; at the time, Chief Merchant Joe Magnacca and his team simply took note of the early signals they were seeing, scrappily filled in gaps in what was offered with brands we'd never carried before, gave it a name and in-store sign, and voilà ... a new department that posted +25 percent sales increases. We expanded refrigerated "doors" and portable energy— everything from grab-and-eat nuts to the first energy bars—because we knew single-serve beverages and on-the-go eating were exploding. We messed with the brand's image, creating a more modern version of the brand identity on the fly, and broke every rule of brand design standards in the process. We started to amplify our "New Yorkness"—the one thing our national rivals couldn't tout—emblazoning the walls behind check-out desks with the slogan "Uniquely New York since 1960," coupled with a tone-on-tone image of the Statue of Liberty. To heck with the folks from Chicago and Rhode Island, we were New Yorkers! (Okay, most of us were Canadians ... but customers didn't know that.)

What customers *did* understand was that the other drugstore options popping up across the city were better in almost every way. Sure, a Walgreens or CVS didn't initially grasp that larger-format packaging sizes wouldn't fly in New York as they do in the suburbs, as most New Yorkers lived in tiny apartments (who knew that ovens weren't for cooking but for shoe storage?). But the "national" stores were cleaner and more organized, the service friendlier and more helpful, and the pharmacies bigger and seemingly more professional. The top executives at Duane Reade knew their proposition and customer experience was in need of a substantial modernization just to close the gap. But field leadership and the majority of head office staff didn't. For nearly five decades they had known nothing but growth and success, and resolutely believed everything was fine just the way it was. "Why on earth would we change? Have you seen how busy the stores are? Have you seen our market share and sales per square foot numbers?" Yet the data told a very different story, revealing a compelling case for change. We needed everyone to grasp that a) the business was in danger, and b) the status quo was *not* an option. I recall Lederer's strong conviction that unless people believed they had to change they simply wouldn't. To him, resistance equaled slow progress when time was of the essence, so getting everyone on board with the "why" was mission critical. With this in mind, we gathered 800 Duane Readers together in an old theater down the street from Madison Square Garden to share the facts we'd uncovered. I recall asking colleagues how plainly we should deliver the hard truths of the situation we were facing, and in this regard I took the advice of COO Chuck Newsome (he a former military man famous for his crisp monogrammed shirts, crew cut, and blunt demeanor): "Joe, you need to leave a smoking hole in that room."

David Saffer was my research guy, and he took the stage that day to deliver the sobering news. Saffer lived a life of gathering data and teasing it to reveal insights, and, like Newsome, he wasn't one to sugarcoat the truth. The data was literally shouting four things, one clarion call for change and three rich insights with enormous strategic potential. First, for New Yorkers, loyalty to Duane Reade could be characterized as "the absence of a better option." Ouch. On a more positive note, the other three were opportunities: New York is a powerful and magnetic idea in and of itself, a brand in the truest sense. While Duane Reade wasn't in that same territory, it was tightly associated with it and woven into the fabric of daily life there. Next, life for New Yorkers is anything but easy, yet easy is what they yearn for. Lastly, by virtue of Duane Reade's ubiquity and market position, it uniquely had permission to *do more, mean more, and sell more*. Of the drugstore competitors, we alone—by birthright and the twin DNA strands of "uniquely New York" and "everything New Yorkers need"—could seize the prize and creatively expand on the core idea of "New York Living Made Easy." These five words became our mantra, the headline of our strategy to win with EASY (convenient access was a starting point) and differentiate through an even more tailored and amplified NEW YORK EXPERIENCE and offering.

Twenty-four weeks into the reinvention of Duane Reade, we had a clear destination in mind and a strategy to take us there, plus a number of runs already on the board. We then began the work of merging strategy with what we were learning from first fast steps, and fully set out on the exciting journey to the outcome we defined: build America's best urban drugstore. It was a mission now guided by insights and a simple, actionable strategy, and enabled by the complete alignment of leadership on where to go and what to do. We believed this would yield a more meaningful place within the lives of New Yorkers, and a strategically defensible position against our suburban chain rivals. It would also pitch into overdrive Duane Reade's perceived value as a potential asset to those very same rivals. Said another way, getting it right for New Yorkers would naturally enhance the value of the business *and* make it an attractive acquisition target for a drugstore player trying to figure out how to grow within the "vertical density" of big cities across America.

While we were moving fast from the outset, making changes and experimenting, the pace of change accelerated further with the completion of strategy and what we named our *momentum map*, a step-by-step action plan designed to accelerate the reinvention. Our philosophy was simple: thirty days wouldn't go by without something significant we could launch or amplify to customers and the market as a proof point of our moving closer to becoming the "New York Living Made Easy" company. Every decision we made was filtered by strategy: "Does it make things easier?" and, if so, "Will it contribute to a uniquely New York experience?" If the answers were "yes," then move forward. If "no" or "not really," then we killed it. We tied every decision and action back to strategy, and the effect was to aggregate and therefore amplify every move.

It doesn't get any better than having a tight filter to align "everything and everyone." With this clarity we went after reshaping Duane Reade like our hair was on fire: a brand-defining store in Herald Square across from Macy's was the first to fully showcase the retooled "How I Look" beauty offering and experience under the new brand name "Look Boutique." On the strength of that store design and expert service proposition—in the form of on-staff beauty consultants—Joe Magnacca had convinced some of the sexiest brands in beauty to sell to us, brands that had once flatly stated, "We wouldn't be caught dead in a Duane Reade store." We created new private brands like "Delish"—an expression we kept hearing when we asked New Yorkers how they would describe good food. Delish became a powerhouse lineup of New York–inspired premium food items you just couldn't buy anyplace else. We also created "Apt 5," a line of everyday gadgets and solutions designed for the realities of apartment living, and a "no name" line we dubbed New York Skyline for its bar code–style graphic illustrations representing iconic images of the city. We built a serious food offering from snacks and sandwiches to fresh-cut fruit and sushi that, store by store, demonstrated that New Yorkers could and would actually eat in a Duane Reade, and in doing so we upped the frequency of visits and emotional attachment to the brand.

We went to work with the agency we had chosen to give us a unique New York voice in the marketplace, and you couldn't get more New York than the ad firm DeVito/Verdi—a couple of New Yorkers through and through and their team of young creatives. They gave us the creative communications platform "Duane Reade. Your City. Your Drugstore." and delivered one memorable headline after another to grace subway signs and billboards popping up across the urban landscape:

"Duane Reade. Where the toughest people buy the softest toilet paper."
"For the city that never sleeps, we have something for that too."
"Germs are everywhere. So are we."
"Duane Reade. How to survive on an island."

We had not only found our voice, we had found our audience. With every wave of the campaign, with every new brand launch, with every new or renovated store, piece by piece we rebuilt the image, offering, and experience of the new Duane Reade. New Yorkers responded with their purses and wallets. Traffic went up. Sales went up. Margins went up. Within two years, Duane Reade went from one list—the worst of New York evidenced by the daily list of grievances posted online—to another, *New York Magazine*'s annual "Best of New York" list. A two-page spread in the *New York Times*, extolling the virtues of the surprising reinvention of Duane Reade, marked a turning point in how the brand was seen and valued by New Yorkers, and became a source of huge pride for every Duane Reade employee. Fortunately, amongst the article's readers were the future buyers of the business, and it too helped to change how they perceived and valued the business.

In the autumn of 2009, Greg Wasson, CEO of the giant Walgreens company, arrived in Manhattan with his team, all wearing jeans and baseball caps. They kept hearing from their New York field team (and reading in the press) about Duane Reade's gravity-defying transformation and fanned out across every updated store they could find. By mid-afternoon Wasson had seen enough. He called everyone together in an uptown location and said, "These folks are on a roll and doing something we've never seen before. There's a lot to learn here, and I seriously doubt we can win against them in New York. We should consider buying them." Duane Reade was sold to Walgreens on April 9, 2010, and when Lederer introduced us to Wasson some months later, his first question was, "How the heck did you folks go so fast?"

The point of this story? There are five points actually, the five principles of the Reinventionist Mindset, born and first tested in New York City:

1 Seek Insight Everywhere.
2 Embrace Uncertainty.
3 Create the Future Now.
4 Obsess the Outcome.
5 Make Momentum Together.

We did all of these things and kept on doing them until we were successful. And while each principle was important on its own, and their value increased when they were applied together, it was the last one that was ultimately proved to matter most. Past a certain point—when we knew where to go and what to do, when we could see it so clearly it practically built itself—it all came down to how much momentum we could make. The faster we got moving and the more we put in motion, the more unstoppable we became. We refused to let ourselves overthink things or get precious with every decision because we knew it wasn't a moon shot; it was okay to be off by a degree or two at the outset and course correct as we went. Why? Because we knew instinctively there was something far more important than making things perfect: MOMENTUM. We knew the more we could create critical MASS, and get it moving at a high VELOCITY, the more we could conjure up this magical cultural and market energy that would speed us all to the promised land. And it did.

DO: A manifesto

At my company Jackman Reinvents, we have a **DO Manifesto**. I'm happy to share it with you with the hope it inspires more doing and less talking about doing.

DO.

It's not enough to think critically and clearly, we must **do**. Doing is what translates powerful insights, ideas, and creativity into value: human value, cultural value, financial value.

It's not enough to do, we must **do well**. The only way the world can fully understand and value our intentions is for us to do our best. Our craft, in every detail and nuance, must always live up to the highest standard. Our standard.

It's not enough to do well alone, we must **do well together**. Individually we are powerful; together we are unstoppable.

It's not enough to do well together, we must **measure to always do better**. Our impact must be understood and learned from so we can continually hone our abilities and grow.

When we do these things, and hold up our **DO** as who we are and what uniquely defines us, we will make our most ambitious dreams a reality. So let's do. Boldly, daily.

PART THREE

MAKE CHANGE

21

The four pillars of reinvention

B EING A PART of the reinvention of companies and their brands is both a privilege and a responsibility. While I find a great deal of joy in it, and it's almost always an insanely thrilling ride, I take it very seriously, as there is a lot riding on the outcome of each. While I never mistake who actually owns the outcome—CEOs and their leadership teams—I always feel beholden to it and to them. The way I see it, for as long as we are at it together, we are in it together. This sense of shared ownership is by design, one of four pillars—or four M's—of reinvention. Though they were developed for my business, they are equally applicable to yours. They are:

Mix. The complete set of skills and experience required for business reinvention, residing under one roof or at least assembled as one cohesive team, and their knowing how to work together.

Method. The collection of steps the team will need to move through together, what we refer to at Jackman as the "Reinvention Playbook," a version of which has been adapted for this book and is included at the end (the Reinvention Workbook).

Mindset. The five principles of how to think and behave throughout reinvention to increase the odds of success—what I have shared with you in the book so far (overviewed in chapter three, and then detailed in chapters five, eight, eleven, fourteen, and seventeen).

Model. The term "model" in this instance refers to some kind of financial model, at minimum a way in which everyone involved in your reinvention will feel they have some ownership of and stake in the outcome. This is the most powerful alignment and motivating mechanism you can deploy.

In this last regard, most senior business leaders already have a real stake in the outcome, through vehicles like stock options, RSUs, or actual shares, which provide a huge financial incentive and motivation. But a key to reinvention is having *everyone* within an organization in some way experience that same sense of ownership, with or without an actual financial stake. The more connected and invested everyone feels the more likely the outcome is achieved, and sooner.

If you are contemplating a substantial transformation of any kind, here's how to apply the four M's to your situation:

Mix. Make sure you have the right people around you, both in regard to skills and temperament. Diversity of thought is a good thing unless it will prevent ultimate alignment. It's always better to have as close to the full team in place at the outset—but don't use assembling the perfect team as an excuse for putting things off. You can always fill in talent gaps as you go. And when you do recruit new players midway through the journey, be sure to invest time into bringing them up to speed and getting their full buy-in to what's already taken place. Better yet, make it a condition of the job offer.

Method. I'll preface how to reinvent a company in the next chapter, and then provide a step-by-step guide in the enclosed Reinvention Workbook. It's as straightforward and as user-friendly as I can make it without turning it into a textbook.

Mindset. You've learned the five principles of the Reinventionist Mindset: Seek Insight Everywhere, Embrace Uncertainty, Create the Future Now, Obsess the Outcome, and Make Momentum Together. I strongly encourage you and yours to live by them as much as possible. Interpret and apply them in any way that feels right to you but live them just the same. I'm offering you a chance to learn from my successes as well as my shortcomings so that you have a better shot at achieving your own outcome. Take it.

Model. This may take some figuring out depending on how you are structured, yet it is well worth the effort. The easiest option: if you can, cut everyone in on the win. In one way or another, make sure they receive a financial reward if you are successful. I did it with my own company, basing my model on taking real equity in the outcome. When we win with a reinvention, every one of my full-time employees has a stake in the payout. It's the best alignment mechanism you could ever imagine.

If you're not able to do this, i.e., put in place an actual financial mechanism, then bring people in on the win in other ways:

- *Make it about them and what they do.* Each day and every step of the way, make sure they know it's only possible if you are all acting together.

- *In a genuine way, appeal to the pride they hold in themselves and the brand.* We all want to be part of something significant and successful, and the outcome will be something everyone will be proud of.

- *Show progress and name names.* Shout out the successes and celebrate those responsible for them. It takes some extra effort, but it's worth it. And, reward those making substantial contributions with promotions, sooner than later.

- *Share the spoils along the way.* While there may not be an actual stake in the business for everyone, sharing the financial wins in some way counts. Whether it's buying everyone a celebratory lunch at a milestone moment, or more substantial rewards like cash bonuses or an unexpected day off. These actions say, "We are making real progress, and the credit goes to you."

22

Reinventing your company

N O DOUBT YOU have gathered I have a bias toward action. I like to *do*. While I enjoy the intellectual and creative work of defining the way forward for any business, the hands-on work of making change happen is the most exciting for me. How wonderful to see the pieces and parts and people coming together into a cohesive and more purposeful whole, a better version of what had existed previously. There is a lot to love about it:

I love the intense focus and energy it requires.

I love the teamwork and the breakthroughs that result from collaborative effort.

I love the early results that prove the thinking or push it further.

I love the momentum that builds—*bang* followed by *bang*—until you can feel the wind rushing by.

I love the results. The satisfaction of seeing a sales trajectory lifting off and the financial value of a business climbing with it.

Most of all, I love how the people involved are themselves transformed. How their demeanor changes from cautious to confident. From down-and-out to up-and-away.

The human FROM/TO in reinvention can be stunning. Depending on the state of the business at the outset, and how long it has been underperforming or in decline, the mood of people within organizations chasing growth without success ranges from fatigued and wary to completely freaked out. At the start everything feels heavy. To witness this dissolve into lightness and positivity—to see confidence and mojo return—is amongst the greatest rewards of reinvention. Those who have experienced it will attest to how deeply satisfying the feeling is. There is nothing better than winning after losing. There is no greater bond than that formed between people who have faced adversity together and overcome it. The very best thing about *down* is that it makes *up* that much sweeter.

Along with the feeling that comes with achieving something worthwhile, reinvention is a compelling commercial proposition. It creates economic value in which everyone can share. A rising sales curve. Growth followed by more growth and opportunity. Expansion. Who wouldn't want to achieve these kinds of results? This kind of motivation is primal. We *need* whatever we are involved in to be successful because our livelihoods and the livelihoods of others depend on it. In another time, it might have meant the difference between catching dinner or going hungry. Now, for most of us, we need to make things work within organizations so we can provide a living for ourselves and our families. It doesn't get much more primal than that.

I'm sharing some of the motivations for reinventing a business because motivation is fundamental to doing it. You are going to need to tap into yours. And you are going to need to appeal to others to tap into theirs. It's hard work to reinvent a company, and not without risk. Despite many successes I, too, have had failures, and out there in the world at large there are, unfortunately, a disproportionate number of those. You do not want to be one of them. The true first step in reinvention is to motivate yourself to undertake it. Get clear on what's ahead and be 100 percent honest with yourself—at the start and throughout. If you are not up for leading change, then step aside. Otherwise you will not make it.

When you are motivated to lead or contribute to a reinvention—choosing to be part of the future by shaping it hands-on—you are on your way. Beyond the satisfaction and rewards that are there for you, ultimately you are going to be a stronger and more capable person at the end of it. Now, you just need to know how to do it.

The most efficient and effective way to reinvent a business

We've talked about the Mindset Principles—the way to think and behave throughout reinvention that will increase your chances of success—and now I'm going to outline *how* to reinvent step by step. You'll find this step-by-step method in the enclosed Reinvention Workbook. Understand that the mindset and method are consciously designed to work together—the yin and yang of reinventing.

My goal with the Reinvention Workbook is to make the steps as simple as possible, enabling you to:

- Build a foundation of facts and feelings
- Make a case for change and a case for confidence
- Uncover insights
- Define an aspirational and financial outcome
- Make strategic choices on how to achieve it
- Bring your strategy to life through bold creative concepts
- Activate your strategy across all internal and customer touch points

Everything you do in reinvention will lead to maximizing momentum (remember we talked about that) and value creation, working much like a high-performance automobile: sourcing the fuel you will need for the journey; setting the course; gaining traction and generating greater and greater speed as you go. In any kind of reinvention this is what you want on your side: more force (alignment of people and plans); more traction (the actions you take, coupled with hitting the gas); and all of it guided by a simple steering mechanism (your strategy). When you break that down into a firing sequence, there are nine important moments, which I've identified as nine straightforward steps to getting any business back to growth and a sustainably strong strategic position. These are the same steps my team and our partners go through every time we undertake a reinvention.

A few last notes before you use the Reinvention Workbook

You will recall I talked about, in chapter twenty-one, having the right *mix* of people involved, and putting in place some kind of a *model* or financial incentive that ties them to the rewards of reinvention. Thinking through and getting organized in these ways *before* you begin a reinvention will set you up for success. Do not use this as an excuse for delay, just get ready as best you can before you begin.

23

Becoming
a pro
athlete of
change

"What you can do, or dream you can, begin it;
boldness has genius, power, and magic in it."

JOHANN WOLFGANG VON GOETHE
(translated by John Anster)

WHEN I FIRST finished the draft manuscript for this book, I shared it with my editor Paul Taunton, my content collaborators Roberta Albert and Megan O'Farrell, and a few colleagues at work. Up to that point it was a business book, full stop, as this is what I had set out to write. Yet, as feedback came back, a surprising theme emerged: *Can you make it personal?* Beyond telling real-life stories and drawing from them lessons applicable to businesses and their reinvention, why not add a chapter to show how the principles could be applied to people and their lives? In other words, a "how-to" for those wishing to reinvent *themselves.*

Hmmm.

I wondered if I could possibly do that in an authentic way, and whether anyone would find it credible, if indeed helpful. I wondered if I would risk being seen as some kind of wannabe life coach and pop psychologist instead of a professional Reinventionist. Definitely not my aspiration. For me, just writing a business book was a leap in and of itself—so why would I want to take that chance?

Can you see it?

Right there, in that moment, is the very crux of what stands in our way. My deliberation of whether to venture beyond what I knew, what I was comfortable with, is the perfect illustration of what stops us from making change:

Fear of the unknown.

"I'm not sure where this will lead. Hard pass."

Fear of being seen as an impostor.

"What do I know about reinventing lives? Will people take me seriously?"

Fear of failure.

"What if people don't find value in this?"

Fear of going it alone.

"Everyone around me is going to find this a stretch. I would be on my own with this one."

In the context of big life decisions, this example is comparatively light. Yet it does serve as a decent illustration of the reasons we choose *not* to try something. When future possibilities present themselves, as they regularly do, we have a way of tearing them down until they are gone, until we remain safely and comfortably where we are.

But what if the circumstances were different?

What if you or I were truly stuck, and it was a much heavier decision with greater consequence. What if we weren't happy where we were, but simply afraid to try something new or head in a fresh direction. What would that look and sound like?

We would tell ourselves that things aren't really that bad.

We would make excuses, eventually on a daily basis.

We would doggedly avoid the truth.

We would hope for the best.

We would convince ourselves that this is our fate.

We would regularly take no for an answer.

When we attempted to change, we would see failure as proof we are unable or unworthy.

We would put off decisions until, one by one, they were made for us.

We would continually walk to the end of our path—close enough to the edge to catch a glimpse of a possible future, or at least sense there is something there for us beyond—and then we would retreat from it. We would return to our comfort zone.

Or, we would be inspired by and drawn toward it.

We would start asking ourselves *what if* instead of *why not*.

We would consider where and how we might be our truest and best selves.

We would think about where and how we might do the most good in the world.

We would be open to possibilities. Indeed, we would start seeking them out.

We would imagine the place we could get to.

We wouldn't worry about every step—just the next one. Seldom would we stand still.

We would ask for help and freely give ours to others.

We would count our losses as lessons, and our lessons as permission and encouragement to go further.

We would accept that it is completely fine and normal to be fearless and fearful at the same time.

We would believe in ourselves and understand the power that flows from that. As Goethe also wrote, "Magic is believing in yourself, if you can do that, you can make anything happen."

And, we would learn to love change. We would see it not as a bad thing but as a good thing. A human skill there to be mastered.

If we did these things, you and I, in the end we would be Reinventionists. We would set ourselves on a path to become pro athletes of change.

This is how I apply the principles of the Reinventionist Mindset to my life. I hope there is value in it for yours.

24

A final thought

FIRST, THANKS FOR staying with this to the end. We made a deal at the outset—that I would share what I have learned, and you would think about how to apply it to your situation. I've done my best to keep my end of the bargain, and I fully expect you to keep yours.

So, let me ask you this; as you think about what's ahead:

Who better to create the next version of your company (or yourself) than you?

If not now, then when?

What's holding you back?

I wish you every success on your journey to Reinventionist.

With appreciation

WHO KNEW THAT, much like building and rebuilding businesses, writing a book would take a village of thinkers and doers. I am so fortunate to be a part of a diverse and supportive community—a group of clients, colleagues, family members, and friends who have inspired, guided, and collectively said, "Heck yes, you can do this." Please indulge me while I shout out a few by name.

John Lederer. Client. Boss. Transformational leader. Mentor. Friend. Inspiration. I have learned so much from working with you, JL. You were the one who never doubted me, gave me every opportunity to learn and grow, and never settled for anything but the utmost from me (thinking, creative, effort, results). You helped me through the very darkest days. I will always be grateful.

Glenn Murphy. From the day you tugged at the back of my head on a store tour when we were young and asked, "Is your hair real?" you've been tugging on my brain and pushing me to hone my skills, think bigger, and deliver faster. I hope to always be in your orbit and will always count you as friend and mentor.

My family. Caterina Jackman, my wife, love, and sage, who listened to every word without complaint and encouraged me to write the way I speak. My children, Lucy, Grace, and Niall, the center of my world and for whom this book is dedicated. My sisters Maureen, Marji, and Barb, who raised and inspired me. My brother, Bernie, who has made me laugh for more than five decades. My warrior sister, Terri, who fought tirelessly for cause after cause and who we tragically lost early. My father, Bill, and mother, Babe, the perfect yin and yang of what's important and possible in life.

My team. David Zietsma and Sandra Duff, who lead my business with drive, smarts, and compassion. My Advisory Chairman and friend David Moore, without whom I could not have built and sustained a business. My unstoppable assistant Jaclyn Drury, who does the impossible daily and makes it look easy. All of the incredibly talented and dedicated people at Jackman Reinvents, who together are changing the world and every day demonstrate what it means to be Reinventionists.

Roberta Albert. Would you have ever thought, back when you were a leader in the marketing department at Loblaw Companies and a client, that some thirty years later you would be my collaborator on a book? I could not. But there you were, week in and week out, relentlessly encouraging me to say it more clearly, get to the point, and just get it done. You are a blessing, Roberta; without you, there would be no book. Wednesdays will forever be marked in my calendar.

Megan O'Farrell. Beware the boss that says, "I have a special project for you." I did, and you delivered. Thanks for the many reviews and comments, and for serving up thoughtful feedback that almost always began with, "I'm not sure you will agree with me on this . . ." I did, even when it didn't sound that way.

Those who inspired and taught me valuable lessons over the years. In alphabetical order: Tony Altilia. Stephen Bebis. Jack Bensimon. Alex Bogusky. David Boone. Stephen Brady. Peter Byrne. Mike Calbert. Tony Chapman. Sandeep Chugani. Paul Clark. Richard Currie. Brian Davidson. Fred Dumais. Bill Durnan. Tracy Fellows. Mark Foote. Mark Frissora. Alan Gertner. Lorne Gertner. Alex Gourlay. Marka Hansen. Hanif Harji. Wayne Hartford. Stefan Kaluzny. Jim King. Steve King. David Lavin. Scott

Lindsay. Allan MacDonald. Joe Magnacca. Alexander Manu. Joe Mimran. Wade Miquelon. Dave Mock. Mike Motz. The Neal brothers. Dave Nichol. Ed Ogiba. J.B. Raftus. Nicholas Reichenbach. Heather Reisman. Frank Rocchetti. Tess Roering. Harry Rosen. David Saffer. Morris Saffer. Mark Satov. Pietro Satriano. Rick Schnall. Stuart Schuette. Frank Scorpiniti. Jill Soltau. Chris Staples. Amanda Stassen. Christian Stuart. John Tavolieri. Joe Teno. Craig Trettau. Terry Tsianos. Bill Wafford. Marshall Warkentin. Greg Wasson. Don Watt. Colin Watts. Cameron Whitworth. Tyler Wolfram. Tom Wyatt. Charles Yao. Iris Yen.

Paul Taunton, Jesse Finkelstein, and Page Two. Your counsel and encouragement were exactly what I needed.

REINVENTION
WORKBOOK

This Reinvention Workbook is structured in two sections:

Creating a four-part framework for reinvention to help you make and align every decision:

- **Own** (which customers to focus on)
- **Win** (how you will attract and keep them)
- **Live** (how you will behave as a brand internally and externally)
- **Category of one** (the outcome you will focus on achieving)

Phase One is completed when these choices are conceptualized and you have a clear outcome in mind.

Engineering a sequence of actions that will ignite momentum and take you to your desired outcome:

- **Activation pyramid** (defining the actions you will take)
- **Momentum map** (developing a plan for sequencing these actions)
- **Execution** (the full implementation of your plan)
- **Reinvention dashboard** (choosing which metrics to measure and tracking your progress)

Working as a team through nine clearly defined steps organized into these two phases of work, Phase One should take you twelve to twenty weeks (depending on the time it takes to gather and analyze data) and Phase Two extends as long as it takes to achieve your outcome. That said, the heavy lifting of reinvention—the Phase Two *doing*—is usually an eighteen- to twenty-four-month undertaking, followed by further scaling and perfecting of the execution.

Before you begin your reinvention, let me explain what I mean by "working as a team." I am a resolute believer in collaboration and have learned that a workshop approach, with full leadership team participation, works best throughout the reinvention process. In Phase One, I recommend a series of all-day sessions for you and your functional leaders—the direct participants in this phase—to come together at natural junctures. In these sessions, you will be sharing and discussing your findings, asking and answering the critical questions laid out in this workbook, and collaboratively developing hypotheses. Each workshop will build upon the one prior, and decisions will naturally crystallize as you move through the sessions. As for how to conduct them, as humorous as it may sound, think back to the Family Meetings I described in chapter one: every participant was considered a peer and on equal footing; the chairperson was nominated on a revolving basis rather than by seniority; tension between points of view was encouraged; full dialogue and honesty were the rule; and humor and camaraderie were the norm. What you are striving for is getting as close to a Socratic forum as possible. The senior-most leader has decision rights, of course, but good ones know that collective will is more powerful than any singular directive.

Step 1. Immerse yourself in your business

Fully reacquaint yourself with your business as objectively as possible, with a fresh set of eyes. Reference chapter five for general guidance on what you are looking for.

Exercise checklist

- [ ] Experience how your business shows up via your sales force, frontline employees
- [ ] Gather physical perceptions (stores, facilities, fleet, collateral)
- [ ] Gather online and other digital perceptions
- [ ] What are customers saying (informal conversations, social media)?
- [ ] What are associates saying (also informal, focused on history and lore of the business)?
- [ ] What are the experts and media saying (read everything)?
- [ ] Look at the category (winners, losers, disruptors)
- [ ] Look at the competition (strengths, weaknesses; do your best to reverse engineer their strategies)
- [ ] Look outside the category (innovation scan)
- [ ] Look into the future (category evolution, macro trends, faint signals)

Step 2. Make a case for change

Build the "why"—why you need to reinvent—based upon the immersion in Step 1. Reference chapter fourteen for a reminder on the importance of doing so.

Exercise checklist

- ☐ List the obvious reasons
- ☐ Go deeper; develop a long list
- ☐ Develop a hierarchy of up to five compelling reasons that together make the strongest case
- ☐ Develop a similar list of reasons you are confident you will be successful, including advantages
- ☐ Memorialize your lists

Step 3. Develop a foundation of facts and feelings

Gather and digest everything you can uncover about your business, your customers, your category, and your competitors: financial performance, performance on key metrics with competitive benchmarks, market trends, spend, growth, customer satisfaction, brand attributes versus primary competitors, innovation and disruptor assessment. Compile a comprehensive summary of facts and feelings that will be foundational to the work ahead.

Exercise checklist

- ☐ Develop customer segmentation (preferably commissioned quantitative research)
- ☐ Probe customer attitudes and behaviors (preferably commissioned qualitative research)
- ☐ Develop market and competitive analysis
- ☐ Conduct full business performance analysis
- ☐ Prepare a key trends report
- ☐ Assess brand health (key attributes, index against competitors)
- ☐ Conduct a market scan for innovation (as benchmarks and inspiration)

Glean insights from everything gathered and digested in Steps 1 and 3: broadly, the patterns, anomalies, and observations that stand out most (what I call the "pings"); more specifically, deep insights into why people/customers are behaving the way they do and what they really want and value. There are many practical ways to uncover insights, such as cultural scans and ethnographies, test and learn initiatives, and simply asking questions and listening carefully. Chapter five is a good refresher on this.

Exercise checklist

Develop a long list, then short list, of what you believe are the most important insights in each of these buckets:

- ☐ Customer
- ☐ Brand/company (including DNA)
- ☐ Competitors (benchmark for old and new)
- ☐ Category
- ☐ Market

Set your strategic direction by making the three most important and interrelated choices: which customers you are focused on and why, how you will win with them, and how you will behave as a brand. The Joann story, told in chapter ten, is a good primer for how this all works together.

Exercise checklist

Own (customer strategy): working with your quantitative customer segmentation, which customer segment will you "own," and from which others will you earn "more than your fair share"? (See Illustration A.)

☐ Which segments are the most engaged in the category?

☐ Which segment truly leads (e.g., first to adopt what's new)?

☐ If you were to fully own the top segment, which others would naturally follow?

☐ Where's the money and growth by segment?

☐ Start with your selection of the top three and push them into a hierarchy; the segment you will "own," two segments from which you will earn "more than your fair share," and the rest.

Win (competitive strategy): how will you win and differentiate your brand with these customers? (See Illustration B.)

☐ On which competitive dimension (i.e., price, quality, assortment, customer service, convenience/access, community, experience) will you truly beat your competitors to win with the customers you've chosen?

☐ Repeat to determine the dimension you will differentiate with, the next level of your competitive strategy

☐ What are the dimensions on which you must compete or be as good as your competitors in order to avoid being deselected by the customers you've chosen?

For each of these three competitive strategy choices—win, differentiate, and compete—define the big actions you will take to bring these choices to life (for example, an Easier & Seamless Customer Experience, or First-to-Market offering), articulated as action blocks that will build your strategy. (See Illustration C.)

Live (brand strategy): who are you as a brand, and how will you show up and behave in the marketplace and within your organization? (See Illustration D.)

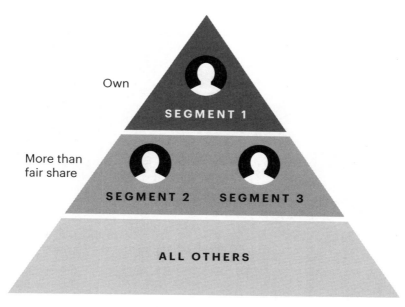

Own

More than
fair share

SEGMENT 1

SEGMENT 2   SEGMENT 3

ALL OTHERS

ILLUSTRATION A

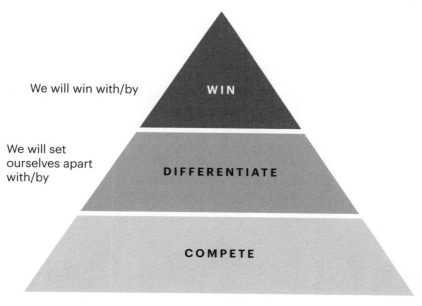

We will win with/by

We will set
ourselves apart
with/by

WIN

DIFFERENTIATE

COMPETE

ILLUSTRATION B

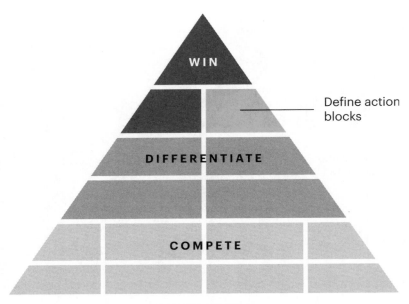

Define action blocks

ILLUSTRATION C

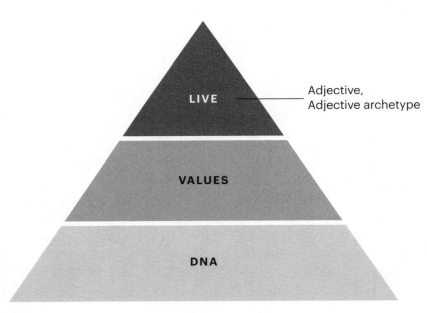

Adjective,
Adjective archetype

ILLUSTRATION D

☐ What are the main strands of your DNA?

☐ What are your values? (If you have a previously defined set of values, examine them in light of the strategic choices you are making; is there a need to update them? Now is the time.)

☐ How do you intend everyone in your organization to behave and live?

The idea of defining your brand as how you and your organization will "live" is powerful: it personifies a brand, defining its character and behavior as if it were *human*. (You won't be surprised to hear from me that humanizing a brand in this way works best.) It is a simple construct: a behavioral archetype, preceded by two modifying adjectives. This may sound abstract, but here are a few real-life examples from companies I have worked with:

- Passionate Scrappy Renegade
- Friendly Clever Ally
- Dynamic Inspiring Partner
- Positive Personal Advocate
- Approachable Make-It-Happen Host

In each of these examples, you can surmise how the entire behavior of an organization is guided in an explicit way, built upon its values and DNA, and tied back to its customer and competitive strategy choices.

For the exercise above, keep in mind my definition of brand: *Brand is purpose, elevated to an experience, delivered consistently.* Brand isn't a logo or communications alone; it is *cultural*—the entire way in which a company behaves and shows up based on who it is, what it values, and its DNA. You will be building a fully formed brand articulation that will shape and guide "everything and everyone."

Step 5 is the heaviest strategic lifting you'll face in the process. Here are a few tips on making the three choices outlined above (Own/Win/Live):

- Make all your choices based upon the full set of facts and feelings and the insights you feel most strongly about. The case for change is a forcing mechanism to ensure you are bold in your choices; keep it handy and refer to it often. My rule is when in doubt, err on the side of boldness. If the idea of going a certain way scares you, it is likely the right path.

- The better you did your homework leading up to Step 5, the sharper and more supportable your strategy will be, and the greater conviction everyone will have that it's right.

- Work and rework your Own/Win/Live choices until they seem to gel with one another. You want a cohesive set of choices, and you'll know it when they make logical sense together *and* feel right.

Step 6. Define and articulate your category of one outcome and BHAG

Next, define the outcome you are working toward, the place where the three strategic choices made in Step 5 will lead (recalling the idea of "promised land"). You want both an aspirational destination (how you will describe your category of one) and the big, hairy, and audacious financial goal (BHAG) you intend to achieve.

Exercise checklist

☐ Write your own FROM/TO: describe the category you are in today—the FROM—and the one you are about to create—the TO—which will become your unique category of one.

☐ Set a BHAG, your new financial goal: ideally a top-line revenue number and bottom-line profit percentage by a certain year (e.g., $20B @20% × 2023).

In this exercise, it may be helpful to reference the FROM/TO of either Joann in chapter ten (FROM: a fabric and craft retailer > TO: the Handmade and Shared by You Company) or Duane Reade in chapter twenty (FROM: a local drugstore > TO: the New York Living Made Easy Company).

Step 7. Picture the outcome and map your momentum toward it

Now, based upon the choices you have made up to this point, illustrate what your future will look like in as tangible a way as possible—through words, images, concept drawings, financial models—whatever it takes to make the outcome clear and compelling in everyone's mind. Then determine the high-level sequence of actions you will take to maximize momentum.

Exercise checklist

☐ Create a conceptual presentation of what your organization will look like within three years, the end state conjured up as powerfully as you can make it.

Include the transformation of your products and/or services, what your digital experience will look and feel like, how your stores or other physical assets will be designed, and your brand image—all your key customer touch points. If possible, show all of the above as before/after images and put them together with a short narrative of where your company is going.

☐ Build your momentum map.

Working with the blocks and key initiatives from Step 5, build out the optimal progression of events, showing when significant initiatives will be launched over the next twenty-four months. You are setting the plan and timing that everyone will follow, and your objective is to *maximize momentum*. Think about what changes you might make to timing and sequencing to generate more force in changing the performance trajectory and changing people's minds. Reference the Duane Reade story in chapter twenty to refresh on the concept of a steady cadence of actions that builds momentum and changes perceptions and performance *fast*. As a draft momentum map emerges, push harder on what can be done even faster.

Having completed Phase One, Steps 1 through 7, you now have a complete category of one strategy to guide the reinvention of your business.

The Jackman Reinvents category of one strategy

To give you an idea of what the output from Phase One of the Reinvention Workbook looks like, here is the Jackman Reinvents strategy.

Which customers are we focused on? Future-forward leaders.

How do we win with them? The mix and mindset of our *people* create the fastest route to value creation; our unique *method* is the differentiator.

What are the DNA strands of the brand? Balance facts and feelings. Hands-on change. Everything is possible.

What are our values? Respect. Empathy. Partnership. Optimism. Courage. Initiative.

How do we live as a brand? Bold magnetic doers.

What is our category of one? The world's first and foremost reinvention company.

What is our BHAG? Sorry, this is confidential. But I can share that it was just reset as a three-year goal to 2023, and it gets our blood flowing.

You can spot how each of these elements is in some way interconnected. It hangs together as a whole and is very precise in how it guides every decision. While every element is important and interrelated, it is the *live* statement that matters most to everyone in my company. It breaks down like this:

Bold: The standard of thinking and work to which we hold ourselves accountable and a direct reference to the *future-forward leaders* we are focused on. It's what they expect from us.

Magnetic: There is only one way to create the future, and that is together. When we collaborate, everything becomes magnetic and draws us forward.

Doer: Action is what creates momentum and achieves results, not talk and intentions. Ours is a bias toward purposeful action, and this really resonates with our customers and amplifies our differentiation.

PHASE TWO

As you begin Phase Two, the circle of those involved will naturally get wider. In Phase One, it was you and your leadership team at the core; functional leaders at levels below were brought in as you worked through activation planning—for example, defining initiatives within action blocks to bring your strategy to life. Phase Two requires full engagement of the organization: building detail into plans, readying and deploying resources for execution, and ultimately engaging with everyone within your organization to build a groundswell of action and momentum. It is the most exciting phase of reinvention in my view, for all the reasons I outlined at the start of chapter twenty-two. You have figured out where to go, and now it's time to get everyone going there together.

Step 8. Tell the world

You have set your strategy and ambition. You have pictured where it is going to take you. You know what to *do*. And, as a leadership team, you are 100 percent aligned and excited to create the future. Now you need to bring everyone fully on board and get them to lean forward into the work and in the same direction.

This step calls on you and your team to simplify and hone the *articulation* of your strategy, craft your main messages for each audience, and immerse them in your strategy to the level of detail as appropriate to their role. Keep in mind the more you share, the more it becomes *their* strategy, too. What you want is every associate and every stakeholder, every Board member and vendor partner, you and your customers onside and enthusiastically supportive of your reinvention. This, too, you must do as a team.

Exercise checklist

☐ Craft the simplest and most compelling articulation of your strategy and plan in presentation form and narrative (the "script")

☐ Build a presentation of the conceptual realization you developed in Step 7, a 360-degree view of what the future holds directionally

☐ Create an associate and stakeholder engagement plan and execute it: town halls, regular updates in person and by email, posting progress to the associate intranet, sharing major announcements in advance, circulating media coverage—and don't stop doing it (refer to the sidebar "How to successfully communicate through reinvention" on page 127).

Step 9. Relentlessly execute, measure, and share progress

This last step is about getting it done, choosing what to measure, then measuring the heck out of it so you can understand what's working and where improvement is required. Just as important (or more), it involves regularly sharing this information to a wide audience so everyone sees and feels the momentum and has a scorecard (as noted in Step 8) with which to motivate themselves.

Exercise checklist

☐ Create a detailed plan.

For each initiative within the action blocks, assign an owner and team that will be held accountable for building a tight plan and executing it. Be disciplined about hitting timing expectations and target improvements toward your outcome. Remember that while you are ensuring realization of individual initiatives designed to ladder up to a cohesive transformation, at the same time you are orchestrating how all the pieces and parts come together to create momentum.

☐ Develop a tracker document.

You need to track the action blocks and the initiatives within using red, yellow, or green to indicate the status of each. Have your teams update and review this document with the full leadership team on a regular basis, ideally monthly in at least the early going stages. On a quarterly cadence, regroup with your entire leadership team to take stock of progress, review trackers, discuss and align on the refinement of executional elements, and assess your collective fidelity to your strategy. This last point may sound obvious, but the further out you get from establishing a strategy, the greater likelihood individuals will stray from it. Do not allow that to happen.

☐ Define the most important metrics.

Identify metrics, both hard and soft, that will track progress. Roll it up into a simple dashboard that consolidates measurement into one easily digestible format, a document your team will update and access frequently to understand the progress you are making.

☐ Annual regroup.

Conduct a company-wide regroup on an annual basis to share and show progress, to discuss lessons learned and how they have been applied, and to articulate calibrations to the plan and reset expectations for the year ahead.

Having worked through these phases and steps as a team, you are now on your way to a successful outcome. Do not be daunted when execution plays out differently than you had imagined at the outset; just keep your course and keep moving. Your success rests on three things now:

1 Learning from everything you put in motion, and continually riffing and refining it.
2 Keeping everyone together on strategy and moving forward at a pace.
3 Relentlessly focusing on, and courageously driving toward, your outcome until you reach it.

About the author

Joe Jackman is the CEO of Jackman Reinvents, the world's first and foremost reinvention company. An advisor to consumer brands, retailers, B2B companies, and private equity partners for more than thirty years, Joe has proven invaluable to leaders intent on sharpening strategy and orchestrating insight-led reinventions of their businesses. Throughout his career as strategist, creative director, marketer, and Reinventionist, he has helped companies create the *most powerful and relevant versions of their brands and businesses* in record time; he is widely considered to be the leading expert on rapid reinvention. Joe lives in Toronto, Canada; works across North America; and lectures around the globe.

joejackman.com | jackmanreinvents.com